# Races, Reforms, & Policy

# Races, Reforms, & Policy

*Implications of the 2014 Midterm Elections*

**EDITED BY**

Christopher J. Galdieri

Tauna S. Sisco

Jennifer C. Lucas

The University of Akron Press
Akron, Ohio

All Material Copyright © 2017 by The University of Akron Press
All rights reserved • First Edition 2017 • Manufactured in the United States of America.

All inquiries and permission requests should be addressed to the publisher, The University of Akron Press, Akron, Ohio 44325-1703.

ISBN: 978-1-629220-69-7 (paper)
ISBN: 978-1-629220-70-3 (ePDF)
ISBN: 978-1-629220-71-0 (ePub)

A catalog record for this title is available from the Library of Congress.

The paper used in this publication meets the minimum requirements of American National Standard for Information Sciences—Permanence of Paper for Printed Library Materials, ANSI Z39.48–1984. ∞

Cover design and illustration: Tyler Krusinski

*Races, Reforms, and Policy* was typeset in Minion with Helvetica Neue display by Amy Freels, printed on sixty-pound natural, and bound by Bookmasters of Ashland, Ohio.

# Contents

# Introduction

# Races, Reforms, and Policy
## Implications of the 2014 Midterm Elections
*Christopher J. Galdieri, Tauna Sisco, and Jennifer Lucas*

Every election matters, but every election matters differently. Presidential elections set the terms on which politics will take place for the next four years; who is president affects the nation's policy agenda, the conduct of foreign affairs, and the composition of the federal courts. Midterm elections, on the other hand, are in many ways reactions to a sitting president's administration. In 1966 a strong Republican showing indicated that Americans were becoming dissatisfied with President Lyndon Johnson's handling of the war in Vietnam and his Great Society programs. In 1998 Democrats' unexpectedly strong performance suggested that the public was less interested in President Bill Clinton's affair with Monica Lewinsky than Republicans and inside-the-Beltway media were. Republicans' victories in 2002 were taken as a sign of support for President George W. Bush's handling of the war on terrorism and the impending American-led invasion of Iraq, while the Democrats' retaking of both houses of Congress in the 2006 midterms demonstrated how much Americans had soured on Bush and his leadership.

Under President Barack Obama, the 2010 midterms were no different. Republicans took back control of the House of Representatives, picked up seven seats in the Senate (though they still fell short of a majority), and won governorships and state legislative seats throughout the country. At the national level, politics turned into a series of stalemates and standoffs between the White House and House Republicans; at the state level, revitalized Republicans began passing laws dealing with labor rights, abortion restrictions, and other conservative policy priorities, while drawing congressional and state legislative district lines to increase their chances of maintaining control of the House and state legislatures. The reelection of President Obama in 2012 did little to change the parameters of American politics; while Democrats increased their Senate majority by two seats and picked up a handful of seats in the House, the president's efforts to pass legislation addressing climate change, immigration reform, and gun control were stymied in Congress.

The result was that Republicans did extremely well in 2014. They won nearly every close Senate race and won control of that chamber, expanded their House majority, and all but one of the 2010 class of Republican governors won another term. Why did Republicans do so well, and what does that mean for American politics? In essence, how and why do midterms matter? In March 2015, scholars gathered at the New Hampshire Institute of Politics at Saint Anselm College to consider not just what had happened on Election Night 2014, but what those results suggest about the direction of American politics. The chapters in this volume are refined and revised versions of select papers presented at our conference, the second such postelection conference held at Saint Anselm College. The authors include some who are well-known scholars and others who are at the very beginning of their careers. Some take broad overviews of the election and others focus on very specific tactics or techniques used in the election. Most are political scientists, but some are scholars who study communications or sociology. Some perform historical analyses, while others examine the content of campaign communications, and others deploy sophisticated statistical models. The variety of our authors and of the methods they use to study the 2014 election and its consequences is, we believe, one of the strengths of this book, and makes the volume a deeper and richer analysis than it otherwise would be.

We have organized this volume into four sections. The first is "Overview and Trends," which features two broad analyses of the 2014 Midterm

Election. Robert Erikson examines the results of the elections for the House of Representatives and concludes that Republicans won not just because of short-term factors, such as being the out-party during a midterm election year, but also thanks to the favorable 2010 redistricting in many states, the benefits of incumbency, and the nationalization of congressional elections. He concludes that, for Democrats, a House majority may be out of reach until they are once again the out-party running in a midterm election year during a Republican presidency (which means we will keep an eye out for their chances in 2018). Chad Kinsella and Scott Sedmak consider the Republicans' tremendous success at winning state legislative seats in 2014. They explain Republicans' unprecedented state legislative officeholding, the states where Republicans are still underperforming compared to the presidential level, and the policy consequences of those actions.

Chapters in the second section, "Up Close and Personal: State Level Races," focus on how the 2014 midterm campaigns played out at the state and local levels. In chapter 3, Robert Crew, Jr., Alexandra Cockerham, and Edward James III examine how the Democrats won Florida's second congressional district in a year when they were losing so many other seats nationwide. Emily Wanless studies South Dakota's Senate race, which featured an unusual three-candidate field in the race to succeed outgoing Senator Tim Johnson. Adam Myers examines the North Carolina Senate race, in which Thom Tillis defeated incumbent Democrat Kay Hagan, and suggests that President Obama's decision to delay taking executive action on immigration may have sunk Hagan's chances—despite the conventional wisdom that such action would make it harder for Hagan and other first-term senators to be reelected. And using textual analysis, Jerome Day, Tauna Sisco, and Christopher Galdieri examine the carpetbagger rhetoric surrounding Scott Brown's attempt to cross states lines from Massachusetts to New Hampshire and be elected to the Senate in a second state.

The midterm electoral process is further analyzed in the third section, "Voting Process." Both chapters focus on the issue of wait times for voting, which has become an important issue on recent Election Days. Terri Fine and Charles Stewart III consider how well the recommendations of the presidential commission on reducing Election Day wait times were implemented in the 2014 elections. Michael Herron, Daniel Smith, Wendy Serra, and Joseph Bafumi also examine the impact of wait times, with a particular focus on how they affect voters' confidence in electoral integrity.

The final section, "Policy," considers the role of public policy in campaigns in 2014. In chapter 9, Sean Foreman analyzes several cases of competitive Senate elections from across the country, particularly for several Senate incumbents who were first swept into office by the Obama wave in 2008. He analyzes the effect of the president's policymaking on the 2014 elections by examining what role the Affordable Care Act played in shaping the outcomes of several key races. Although the ACA was not the deciding factor in most races, it did play an important role in giving shape to the discontent over the Obama presidency in a few critical states, such as Louisiana and North Carolina, which were imperative for Democrats to win in order to keep the Senate. It also did not help certain challengers, such as Alison Lundergan Grimes, even in places like Kentucky where the state program had been successful. Heather Silber Mohamed also talks about how the politics of immigration shaped the 2014 elections. She examines why the president considered executive action on immigration, and the response by Democratic senators to urge the president to wait until after the election. She also looks at the ways that different constituencies—particularly Latino voters—responded to these events. She notes the ways Democrats struggled to build support among Latinos, while also not alienating white voters on immigration. In the end, Obama delayed executive actions on immigration until after the election, but it did not help moderate Democrats, and may have cost Latino support at the polls. Mark O'Gorman argues that 2014 may have seen the beginning of a new Republican approach to environmental issues and climate change.

Very often, the rush of results on Election Night is understandably followed by a focus on what will happen under the newly elected officials; to the extent that anyone looks back, it is to conduct surface, postgame analyses. The virtue of a volume like this one is that it allows for a more thoughtful and considered empirical examination of not just what happened, but why, and places the election in a broader context. Examining the 2014 election from multiple scholarly and methodological perspectives will expand our understanding of this and subsequent midterm elections.

# Overview & Trends

# Chapter 1

# Understanding the 2014 Midterm Election

*Robert S. Erikson*

For forty years, from 1955 through 1994, the Democratic Party controlled the House of Representatives, winning a majority in each of twenty elections between 1954 and 1992. This was true even though the Democratic Party controlled the presidency for only fourteen of those forty years. Since 1992 the Democrats have won the popular vote in five of six presidential elections. Yet, since 1995 the Republicans have controlled the House for eighteen of the twenty-three years. Thus, we see a reversal of party fortune from one federal institution to the other.

The 2014 election provides the latest example. In this most recent midterm election, Republicans made their best congressional showing in many decades, regaining the Senate while winning the House of Representatives by their biggest margin since 1924, ninety years earlier. This GOP triumph occurred, of course, during Obama's Democratic presidency and during a climate when Democrats were perceived as at least slight favorites to hold the presidency in 2016 with the candidacy of Hillary Clinton. Even as Congress has received record low approval ratings, pundits again place Republicans as favored to hold the House of

Representatives in future elections, perhaps into the next decade. As Charlie Cook, the leading forecaster has put it:

> one would be hard-pressed to find a single objective expert on congressional elections who believes there is any realistic chance that Republicans could lose their majority in the House of Representatives in 2016. Indeed, a pretty credible case can be made that the next decent shot Democrats will have would be in 2022 . . . if then. (Cook 2015)

How could this be? How could the GOP become so inoculated from the threat of defeat in House elections during an era when the Democrats perform better in elections for president? This circumstance is particularly puzzling given the Democrats' earlier forty-year rule, which abruptly ended with the shock of the Republican landslide in the 1994 Midterm Election.

The current partisan landscape of House elections is largely due to how many votes the two parties receive. This is obvious. But institutional factors matter also, channeling the partisan vote into the partisan division of seats. This chapter explores the sources of the vote and the conversion to seats in accounting for the 2014 election outcome, and ventures some speculation about the stability of the Republican success for future elections.

## THE NATIONAL HOUSE VOTE IN 2014

According to numbers supplied by the Federal Election Commission (Leamon and Bucelato 2015), in 2014 the Republicans won 52.9 percent of the major-party vote for the House nationally. This was their third-best showing during the post–World War II years, being surpassed only by the 1946 and 2010 landslides. This degree of success is owed mainly to the fact that the Republican Party is the "out" party, the one not holding the presidency. The out-party almost always gains votes (relative to the previous presidential election) at midterm. Figure 1.1 shows this pattern, for post–World War II elections. The presidential party has avoided this midterm slump only twice since 1878.[1]

In figure 1.1, hollow dots are with Republican presidents and solid dots are with Democratic administrations. Importantly, the out-party does not simply gain relative to two years earlier. The out-party also per-

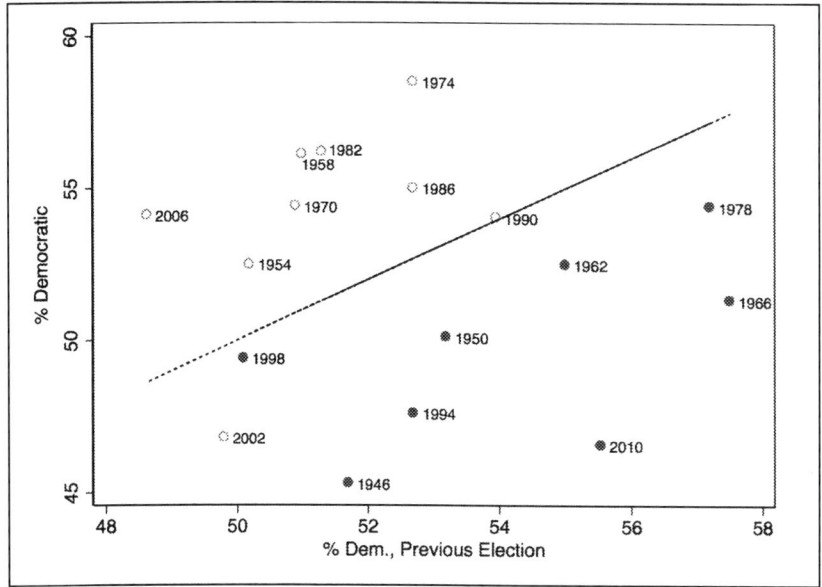

**Figure 1.1.** Democratic Vote for House of Representatives by Lagged Democratic Vote for the House, 1946–2014

forms better at midterm in the absolute sense that its vote percentage tends to be greater in years when it does *not* control the presidency than in years when it *does* control the presidency. In short, if the party's goal is control of the House at midterm, it is good to lose the presidency.

Table 1.1 shows this statistically, with three equations based on post–World War II midterms. The first equation shows simply that the Democratic vote for the House is almost five points greater on average under Republican administrations, a pattern that is highly significant at the .005 level with eighteen cases. The second equation adds party identification, and the third also adds presidential approval, each in October of the election year. (Presidential approval is measured as a deviation from 50 percent; positive under Democratic presidents, and negative under Republican presidents.) With these independent variables added to the equation, the effect of being the out-party holds up, with significant levels beyond .001.

**Table 1.1.** Predicting the Democratic Share of the National Vote in Midterm Elections, 1946–2014

|  |  | (1) | (2) | (3) |
|---|---|---|---|---|
| N=18 elections |  |  |  |  |
| Party of President (1=Democrat, 0=Republican) | Coefficient | -4.82 | -4.33 | -4.86 |
|  | Std. Error | (1.47) | (0.97) | (0.88) |
|  | p-value | [.005] | [.000] | [.000] |
| Party Identification (% Democrat minus% Republican) | Coefficient |  | 0.28 | 0.25 |
|  | Std. Error |  | [0.06] | (0.05) |
|  | p-value |  | [.000] | [.001] |
| Presidential approval minus 50% (minus if president is a Republican) | Coefficient |  |  | 0.11 |
|  | Std. Error |  |  | (0.05) |
|  | p-value |  |  | [.038] |
| Adjusted R squared |  | .363 | .726 | .786 |

Why does the out-party do so well at midterm? One clue is that party identification is very similar on average at midterm under Democratic and Republican administrations. For the most recent nine midterm elections under Democratic presidents, the mean Democratic lead over the GOP in terms of party identification was 12.0 percentage points. Under Republican presidents it was slightly larger at 13.7 percentage points, not enough to make a significant difference. Thus, a party is only marginally less popular when it holds the presidency at midterm than when it does not. So we cannot blame the in-party fortunes on public rejection of the in-party.

Further, presidents are no less popular at midterm than the average approval of presidents over a four-year term. Thus, we cannot attribute the presidential party's midterm failure on a persistent pattern of unpopular presidents at midterm. Only a very positive level of presidential approval—as George W. Bush's in 2002—can overcome the in-party handicap.

*Ideological Balancing?*

The bottom line is that at midterm the out-party does particularly well apart from the standing of the president or the standing of the presidential party with the voters. So what is left to explain the extreme regularity of the presidential party's midterm loss? The best explanation is that midterm electorates engage in ideological balancing (Erikson 1988; Alesina and Rosenthal 1995). The basic idea is that voters consider both the recent and the future policies under the current president. The median voter is to the right (left) of a Democratic (Republican) president. With a Democratic (Republican) president, the way to restore balance is to move policy to the right (left) by electing more Republicans (Democrats) to Congress.

Strong circumstantial evidence supports this claim. Over midterm campaigns, the generic-ballot public opinion polls show the public to be increasingly willing to support the out-party, as if the voters take into account the presidential party as the election nears (Bafumi et al. 2010). Further, regression discontinuity studies of gubernatorial elections show downstream punishment for the governor's party—for the state legislature (Folke and Snyder 2012) or for the governor's party in the next presidential election (Erikson, Folke, and Snyder 2015). When a governor is elected in a close election, the other party benefits downstream, as if to balance the consequences of the gubernatorial outcome.

If the balancing argument is correct, the meaning of the 2014 GOP conquest was not that the public necessarily prefers the ideal policy positions of Republican congressional candidates to those of their Democratic counterparts. Congressional Republicans would overplay their hand if they believe this to be true. Rather, the 2014 voting public preferred a rightward course correction in policy and voting Republican was the vehicle to make this happen.

## TURNOUT AND THE 2014 MIDTERM VOTE

Following the 2014 Midterm Election, a prominent narrative was that the Democrats lost (or lost by a bigger margin than otherwise) because their base voters stayed home rather than voting. Turnout was down in 2014 from two years before, as it is in every midterm election. The usual claim about 2014 is that this decline was proportionately greater for Democratic voters than for Republican voters. Such a relative plunge in Democratic turnout could have resulted because that is what Democrats do in midterms—as voters with lower socioeconomic status, Democratic loyalists are less likely to show up in a lower-turnout election. Or, as is sometimes theorized, at midterm (but only then) the base of the *presidential* party (Democratic or Republican) is typically disillusioned, whereas the out-party supporters are more energized and eager to vote.

Indeed, the 2014 turnout of eligible voters was only 36 percent, the lowest turnout at midterm since 1942 (McDonald 2014). Roughly speaking, turnout among *registered* voters in 2014 was only about 60 percent of what it was in 2012. We must ask, then: Was the midterm electorate much different in terms of vote preference from the shadow electorate who voted in 2012 but not in 2014? We should be cautious in claiming that the answer is "yes."

*Exit Polls, 2012 and 2014*

From exit polls, one can compare the composition of the 2014 electorate with that of 2012. It turns out that these differences are slight. African Americans, the most reliable element of the Democratic base, were 13 percent of the electorate in 2012 and 12 percent in 2014, virtually the same. (Whites, mainly Republican, grew only from 72 percent in 2014 to 75 percent in 2014.) Meanwhile, born-again Christians, the heart of the Republican base, actually shrunk from 20 percent of the electorate in 2012 to 19 percent in 2014. It is true that there was a strong shift in the age composition from 2012 to 2014. Young voters from eighteen to twenty-nine (slightly more Democratic than average) shrunk from 19 percent to 13 percent of the active electorate while elders sixty-five and over (slightly more Republican) grew from 25 percent to 34 percent. Meanwhile, the most pro-Democratic education category, voters with a postgraduate education, expanded from 18 percent in 2012 to 20 percent in 2014.

In short, one cannot tell a consistent narrative in terms of standard demographics whereby the Democrats suffered in 2014 from a systematic disproportionate turnout decline by the Democratic Party base. The one demographic pattern that supports this argument was the age differential, with young voters dropping out while seniors remained steadfast voters. In 2014 the effect of this differential might have had a slightly higher impact on the national vote margin than in past midterm elections, because only in recent elections have young voters become part of the Democratic base. (In earlier elections when young voters had split their votes more like older voters, their lowered turnout had no net impact.)

One comparison of 2012 and 2014 exit polls that should draw notice, however, is the change in the division of party identification. In 2012 Democrats outnumbered Republicans 38 percent to 32 percent in the exit polls. In 2014 Republicans actually outnumbered Democrats 37 percent to 36 percent, for a net seven-point swing. There are two possible explanations. One is that Democrats retreated from voting at a faster rate than Republicans, but not based much on objective demographics. (It would have to be mainly Democrats within each demographic niche who disproportionately dropped out.) The other would be that party identification is sufficiently malleable so that the momentary Republican high tide in November 2014 prompted a temporary surge in self-declared Republican identification.[2]

### The National Vote Margin versus the Mean Vote Margin

The demographic analysis of exit polls casts doubt on the narrative that the Democrats lost in 2014 because their base disproportionately stayed away from the polls. There is still a second reason for caution in attributing the Democrats' poor showing in 2014 to a disaffected base. This reason is the surprisingly low differential between the mean vote margin in congressional districts and the total vote margin in the same districts. The test is as follows. Because Democrats turn out less than Republicans, the national mean Democratic percentage of the two-party vote per district is slightly higher than the Democrats' share of the total national two-party vote. In past congressional election years, this differential has been about 1 percent when the total vote margin is summed only for contested races (Democratic vs. Republican). If the national vote (contested districts) is 50 percent Democratic, for example, the mean vote per district is about 51 percent. Note that this gives the Democrats a slight offset to their lower turnout than Republicans'.

In the presidential year of 2012, the net Democratic percentage of the congressional vote across contested districts was 51.2 percent; the *mean* Democratic vote in the same contested districts was a slightly greater 51.7, modestly reflecting the turnout bias that favors Republicans. In 2014 the Democratic percentage in contested districts declined to 47.0 percent. The mean Democratic vote in these same districts was only 47.2 percent. This trivial 0.2 percent difference is the lowest differential in postwar elections. It means that, on average, there was virtually no difference between the rate of voter turnout in Democratic-voting and Republican-voting districts.

We can see further evidence in figure 1.2, which shows the number of voters per district (smoothed) as a function of the district vote margin

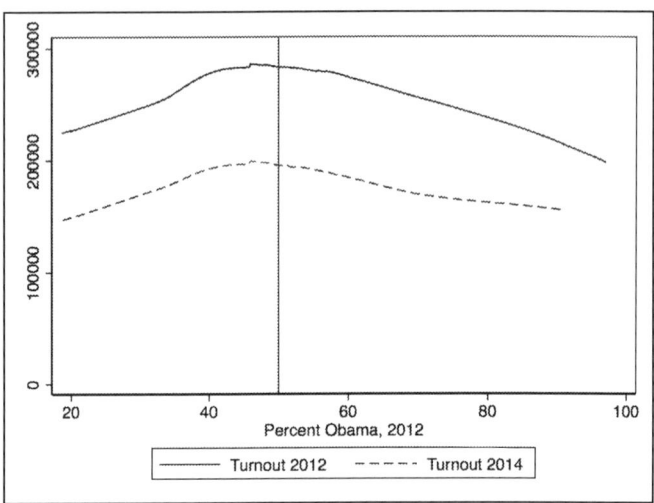

**Figure 1.2.** Voter Turnout in Congressional Elections, 2012 and 2014 as Function of the 2012 Obama Vote

In figure 1.2, the curves are LOWESS curves. The dropoff of the vote in 2014 as a proportion of the 2012 vote is roughly proportional across levels of the Obama 2012 vote.

in 2012 and 2014. Inferred from the number of voters, the voting rate peaks in slightly Republican districts (as measured by the Obama vs. Romney vote). The key takeaway from this figure, however, is that the shapes of the two curves are roughly equal for 2012 and 2014. Democratic districts did not show a meltdown of turnout in 2014 any greater than the decline in GOP districts. This surprising result in terms of aggregates of voters suggests that the differential between the turnout of Democratic and Republican individual voters might have been overstated in 2014.

*Caution and a Puzzle*

It is safe to say that we are left with a bit of a puzzle. The argument here is not to argue against a partisan bias to turnout that helps Republicans. Rather it is that the bias which does exist was not unusually strong in 2014 (and perhaps other midterm elections) compared to presidential years. Speculatively, the lower turnout among Democratic groups (in presidential and midterm years) is a function of potential Democratic voters resisting voter registration. Continuing this speculation, perhaps the reason why Republicans vote more than Democrats is that their more affluent constituents are more likely to register to vote, while once registered different demographic groups vote at similar rates.[3]

## STRUCTURAL FACTORS

In some ways, the 2014 Midterm Election was a perfect storm of structural factors, translating a solid Republican showing in terms of the vote into a decisive control of the partisan composition of the House of Representatives. These factors include:

- The natural Republican gerrymander based on where people live.
- The deliberate Republican gerrymander resulting from the GOP control of most redistricting processes after the 2010 census. (Given both types of gerrymander, the GOP needs less than half the vote to win the House.)
- The inherited GOP congressional majority in 2014. GOP incumbents could benefit from their incumbency to win otherwise competitive seats.
- The 2010 Census–based redistricting equalized district populations, slightly benefiting the GOP.
- The nationalization of elections, which limits the possibility of Democrats offsetting their gerrymander disadvantage with a strong personal vote.

### The Republican "Gerrymander," Natural and Republican-Made

Throughout at least the post–World War II era, elections to Congress have been subject to a natural Republican "gerrymander" (Erikson 1972; Rodden 2010). The word "gerrymander" is in quotes because the distribution of voters across districts favors the Republicans even when district lines are allocated on a nonpartisan basis. The reason is that Democrats tend to cluster in one-party areas, mainly in cities, where their votes go "wasted." The upshot is that Democrats need more than a majority of the vote to win the majority of the seats. This is true today and was also true back during the forty years of Democratic House control. Back then, the Democrats would always get the most votes for Congress. For recent election years, when the national vote is more uncertain and often adverse to the Democrats, the natural gerrymander matters more.

Beyond the natural gerrymander, the 2010 Republican landslide led to many state legislatures being controlled by Republicans, who added their deliberate partisan gerrymandering to the mix. By packing Democrats in one-party districts, while creating GOP seats that were seemingly just safe enough, the Republicans added to their already natural advantage.

We can see this from an analysis of presidential voting by congressional districts. In 2012 Obama's average share of the two-party vote across the 435 congressional districts was a healthy 52.3 percent. Yet he won more than half the two-party vote in only 48.0 percent of these districts. In other words, if the voting rules were like in, say, the UK, where winning requires accumulating more seats than the opponent, Romney would have been declared the winner of the 2012 election. The median Democratic share of the two-party district vote was only 49.1 percent, which is 3.2 percentage points less than the mean Obama margin. To achieve a tie with Romney under the hypothetical rules (and assuming a uniform swing of the vote), Obama would have needed to win 53.2 percent of the vote! Anything less than this, and Romney wins most of the congressional districts!

This bias in favor of Republicans in terms of underlying partisanship of districts is now greater than in past elections, thanks to the one-sided GOP control of the state legislatures that did the redistricting following the 2010 Census. Suppose we make the same calculations for the 2008 presidential vote as we did for 2012. In 2008 Obama would have needed "only" 52.0 percent to win most congressional districts. Thus, the gerrymander burden imposed following the 2010 Census (and in force through 2020) is a shade greater even than that from the 2000s.

Of course, the purpose of gerrymandering is to affect House election margins, not a hypothetical presidential race by districts.[4] Figure 1.3 shows the distribution of the vote across congressional districts in 2014. One can see the evidence of Mayhew's (1974) "vanishing marginals," referring to the low number of competitive districts. What is odd in 2014 is that the vanishing marginals, the nadir between the two modes, is in the range where Democrats barely lost. With few seats where Democrats lost in 2014 but came close, one could conclude that there are relatively few seats for Democrats to gain in future elections.

In 2014 the median district vote margin for the House (218th of 435) was 42.2 percent Democratic, meaning that in half the districts, the Dem-

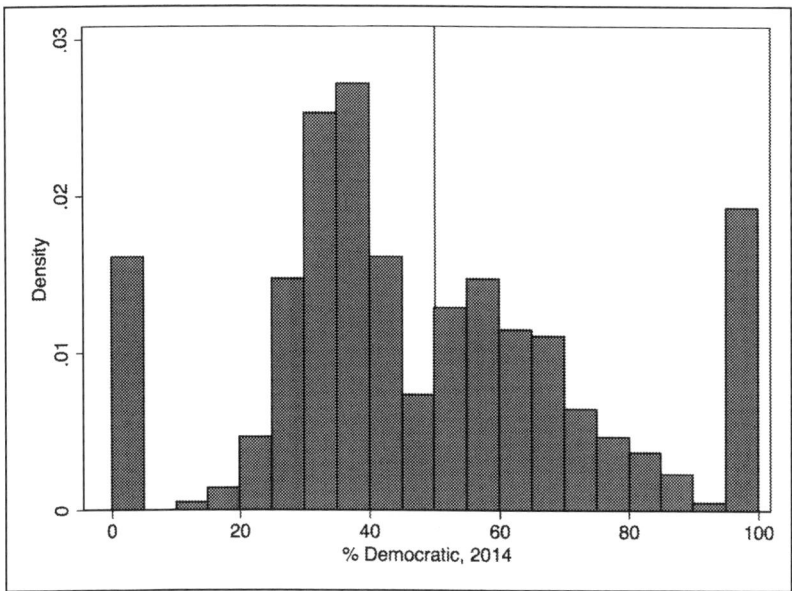

**Figure 1.3.** Distribution of the Democratic Share of the Two-Party Vote in 2014 Elections for the US House

*The distribution is skewed and bimodal.*

ocrats could not win even 42.2 percent of the vote. Yet the Democrats did win 47.1 percent of the total vote. A slightly more relevant comparison number is the estimated mean district vote that would have occurred if both parties ran candidates in all districts. My estimate of this number is 47.3 percent.[5] Thus, if we were to assume a uniform swing of the vote, the Democrats need to win 55.1 (50.0 + 47.3 - 42.2) percent of the two-party vote in the districts created following the 2010 Census. This hurdle is even greater than the 53.2 percent needed to win the most congressional seats in terms of the presidential vote.

*Other Factors: Incumbency, Polarization*

Now we see the predicament facing the Democratic Party when it comes to the House of Representatives. Republicans enjoy the benefit of their gerrymander. Superimposed on this fact is that Republicans start with an advantage of incumbency. Some of their more fragile House seats are in GOP hands thanks to past House victories that are sustained because the new Republican representatives could gain extra votes from their newly found incumbency status. To see why this might be important, consider the following.

In 1964, back in the era when Democrats always controlled the House, Democrats picked up an unusual bonus of House seats due to the shock of the Republicans' nomination of Senator Barry Goldwater for president. This coincided with a growth in the incumbency advantage at about the same time. Many of these new Democratic House members held onto their seats in future elections only with the help of the newly increased incumbency advantage (Erikson 1972; Cox and Katz 2002). Back in 2010, when Democrats held most seats, this incumbency advantage helped to somewhat limit the carnage from the Republican surge. In 2010, the GOP won fewer seats than in 2014 even though they had won more votes. The Democrats kept the damage to less than it would have been under 2014 conditions due to their incumbency as well as the fact that redistricting had not yet occurred.

Complicating matters, recent congressional elections have become more nationalized, with the vote following more from district partisanship than from what the candidates can manipulate in terms of their "personal vote." Congressional elections are not so local anymore. This polarization has aided the GOP in the sense that Democratic incumbents can no longer benefit as much from their personal vote. This polarization also means that candidates can no longer gain as much from their incumbency. In recent elections, the incumbency advantage has definitely declined in magnitude (Erikson 2017; G. C. Jacobson 2015). On the one hand, nationalization of the vote tightens the GOP control. (Consider the outcome if, hypothetically, the House vote mirrored the vote for president.) On the other hand, there may be more churning of seats because the pattern of incumbent protection seems to be breaking.

### THE FUTURE

This chapter began with a speculation about the future. Will, as Charlie Cook surmises, the GOP keep the House into the 2020s? We can speculate that the future might not be as certain as it seems. House elections have been subject to unexpected shocks in the past. Back in 1994, virtually nobody expected the Republicans to win the House despite generic-ballot polls that indicated that they were clearly likely to win the most votes. In 2006 the polls were even clearer that the Democrats led in terms of the votes, yet it was not until the final weeks that observers began to consider that the Democrats might actually take the House back, which they did. The 2010 turnover to the Republicans was a different story, with the outcome telegraphed well in advance by the polls. Yet, even on the eve of the 2010 Midterm Election, not all observers were convinced that the GOP would actually prevail.

No prediction about the future vote will be presented here. However, we can speculate about what would happen if the Democrats were the recipients of a surge in the vote to something like 54 percent of the vote, approximating the outcome of 2006. On paper, a surge to 54 percent would still lead to a GOP majority for the reasons just outlined. Recall the discussion about how, with a uniform swing, the Democrats would have needed a decidedly counterfactual 55.1 percent of the vote in order to obtain a majority of seats in 2014.

But there is reason to think that, conditional on a shift to something like a 54 percent Democratic, 46 percent Republican vote split, the Democrats would win most of the seats. Here is why. The problem with projecting the future division of seats from the current division of seats is that the uniform swing rule is flawed. On the one hand, in 2014 the answer is yes, the Democrats could have achieved a tie in seats if the vote shifted in every district enough for the mean vote to be 55.1 percent Democratic.

In 2014 there were precious few seats where the Democrats barely lost. One important reason was that the Democrats were rationally conceding Republican seats which they could not retake in a Republican year. Instead, the Democrats concentrated their resources into protecting the seats they held. In 2014 there were many seats that, from the vote margin, seemed moderately safe for the GOP but this was partly because the Democrats chose not to compete. This was the "scare off" factor (Cox and Katz 1996). In a future election where the Democrats are expected to gain, the Democrats could place strong challengers and more money in these seemingly Republican seats. They would do better than the uniform swing because the component due to their effort would exceed the effort observed in 2014.

We can see this withdrawal of the scare-off factor in the two most recent surges. If one did a uniform swing calculation in 2004, the conclusion would have been that a surge the size of 2006 would have resulted in a fragile two-seat Democratic majority of about 219 seats rather than the 230 seats that was obtained. Similarly, a uniform swing calculation in 2008 would have underestimated the size of the new GOP seat majority by about two-thirds. In each case, the surging party put renewed effort and gained the most votes in those districts where it saw a chance to take the seat back from the opposition.

While a detailed advance knowledge of the next midterm election in 2018 is unknowable, two very general predictions are possible, one for the Senate and one for the House. For the Senate, the majority of the seats up for election in 2018 are currently held by Democrats (winning them in 2012). Since there are few, if any, vulnerable Senate seats, it is unlikely that the Democratic Party can gains seats in the Senate. For the House, 2018 is another matter. In almost every midterm election, the out-party gains seats. For Democrats looking for a silver lining from Trump's victory in 2016, there is the near certainty that the Democrats will gain seats, rather than the further losses that would have occurred in the counterfactual world in which Hillary Clinton was elected president.

## NOTES

1. The exceptions in terms of votes were 1926 (when the out-party actually lost seats) and 2002 (following 9/11). In 1934 and 1998, the out-party gained seats, but lost strength in terms of the two-party vote.

2. The 2012 to 2014 shift was more modest in terms of *ideological* identification than for party identification. The voting electorate shifted only from 35 percent conservative and 25 percent liberal (2012) to 37 percent conservative and 23 percent liberal (2014).

3. Analysis of voting and nonvoting via the US Census's Current Population Survey shows some support for this view.

4. The allocation of congressional districts to parties based on presidential voting may be academic, but it would become a crucial practical consideration if, as is occasionally threatened, Republican legislatures had changed their states' allocation of Electoral College votes to winning congressional seats rather than the usual winner-take-all procedure.

5. This number is computed by first calculating the Democratic vote share for the House relative to the Obama (2012) vote share in each contested district and then projecting the hypothetical House vote in uncontested districts.

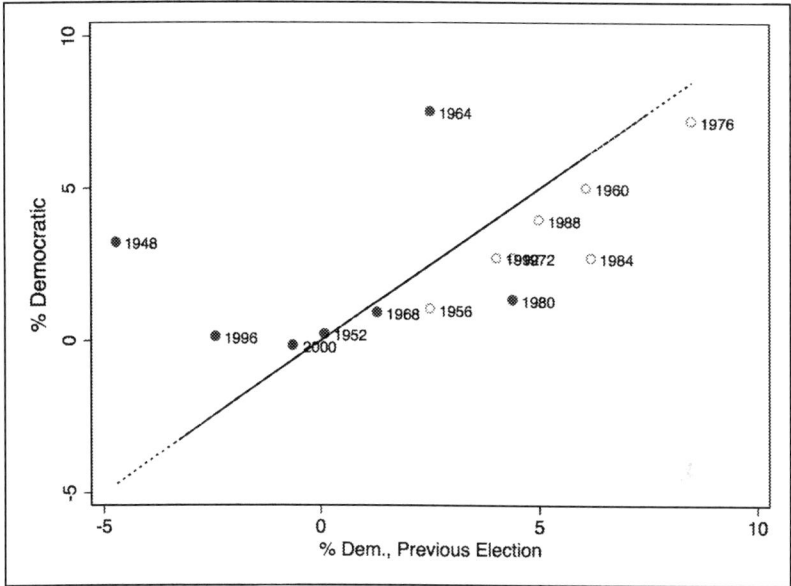

**Figure 1.4.** Democratic Vote for the House of Representatives in Presidential Election Years as a Function of the Lagged Vote, 1948–2012

*Hollow dots are with Republican incumbent presidents. Solid dots are with Democratic incumbent presidents.*

Chapter 2

# The Other Republican Wave
## 2014 State Legislative Elections
*Chad Kinsella and Scott Sedmak*

Overall, pundits and political scientists saw the 2014 Midterm Election as a "wave" election for Republicans. In the case of 2014, Republicans gained nine Senate seats, increased their majority in the House of Representatives, and were not only able to hold several endangered gubernatorial seats, with the exception of Pennsylvania, but also gained governors' posts in the traditionally Democratic states of Massachusetts, Maryland, and Illinois. And Republicans were able to make substantial gains in state legislatures across the country, erasing gains made by Democrats in 2012 and surpassing Republican gains made in 2010. As of 2015, Republicans control an unprecedented 56 percent of the nation's state legislative seats, or 4,128 state legislators out of 7,334, a level of control not seen since before the Great Depression (see fig. 2.1).

In many ways, the 2014 state legislative wave is a continuation of the wave election that occurred in 2010. That year, Republicans regained the US House of Representatives and captured several state legislatures throughout the country, undoing many of the gains made by Democrats in 2006 and 2008. Realizing the importance and potential of the 2010 election, Republicans created and funded several groups to win at the

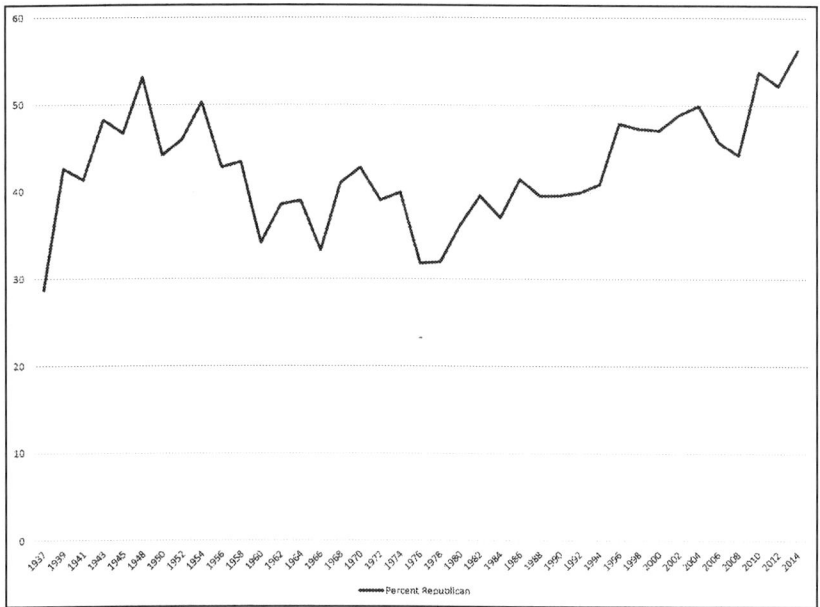

Figure 2.1. Percent of Republican State Legislators, 1937–2015

*Source: Carl Klarner*

state level (Stirewalt 2015). Furthermore, those state legislators elected in 2010 were able to draw the legislative maps in such a way as to, in many states, benefit their respective parties in future elections.

Like 2010, midterm elections historically tend to be poor showings for the party that controls the presidency. Nationally, President Obama's approval rating leading into the 2014 elections was even worse than it was in 2010, with his strong disapproval numbers more than doubling his strong approvals (McCarthy 2014b). The end result of the wave election was a Republican net gain of 248 House seats and 53 Senate seats for a total pickup of 301 state legislators. These pickups resulted in a large number of legislative chambers. As of 2015, Republicans have control of thirty state legislatures, leaving ten in control of Democrats, another nine under split control, and one (Nebraska) officially nonpartisan (see fig. 2.2).

Overall, every region in the country saw an increase in the number of Republican state legislators. The largest gain for Republicans came in the East, where their number increased by over 6 percent. Gains in the

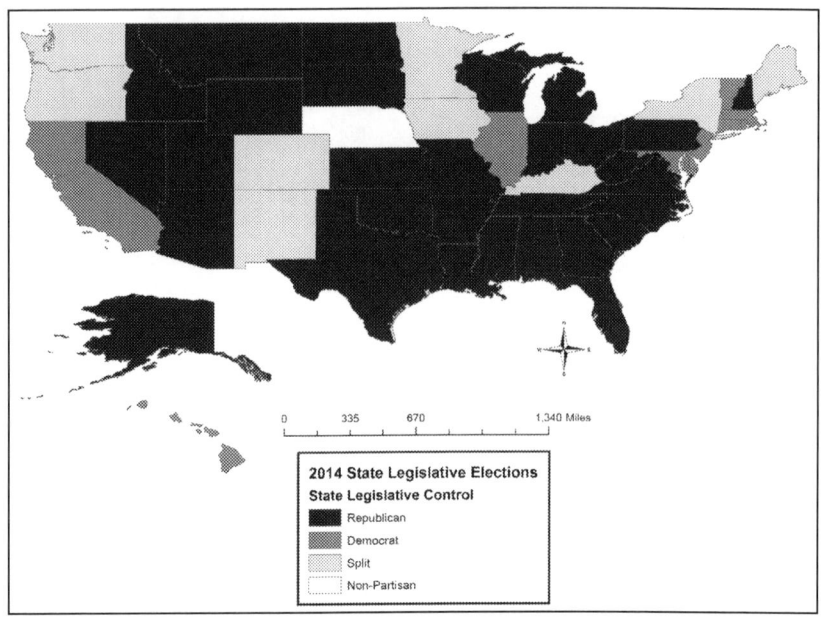

Figure 2.2. Partisan Control of State Legislatures: Post–2014 Election Regional Trends

South and Midwest were about 3 percent each. The Western states saw the lowest gain for Republican state legislators at just over 2 percent.

In 1937 there were only a handful of Southern states that had Republican state legislators, most of them concentrated in the Upper South. Although Southern states began to vote Republican in presidential elections for decades, the ascendancy of Republican state legislators in the South is a recent phenomenon, given that the Republican takeover was a top-down, uneven affair (Aistrup 1996). Now every state legislature in the South, including the border states of Kentucky and West Virginia, has Republican majorities in both chambers.

In the Midwest, the historic home of the Republican Party, gains for the GOP in recent elections make it closer to its historic strength in the region. Currently, it is almost even with the South as having the highest percentage of Republican legislators. Since 2006 there has been a considerable increase in the number of Republican state legislators in the region and, with the exception of Illinois, Iowa, and Minnesota, both chambers of state legislatures in the rest of the Midwest are under Republican control.

The East remains the region with the lowest number of Republican state legislators. Although this region had the highest number of pickups for Republicans in the 2014 election, especially in New Hampshire and Maine, the increase does not replace Democratic gains in 2012. There are several states in this region that have overwhelming Democratic majorities, such as Massachusetts, Vermont, and Rhode Island, which were largely unaffected by the national trend of Republican support.

The Western states were the scene of the Republican wave's greatest successes and failures. Overall, the 2014 Midterm Election replenished Republican losses from the 2012 General Election and increased the percentage of Republican state legislators in the region to over 55 percent. Nevada had the largest increase in Republican state legislators in the country, with a nearly 30 percent increase and the takeover of both chambers of the state legislature. There were only a few states that saw state legislative victories for Democrats in 2014 and all of them were in Western states. Montana, Idaho, Alaska, Oregon, and Wyoming all bucked the national trend and saw net gains for Democrats. Despite this bright spot for Democrats, all the states, except Oregon, have large Republican majorities and, despite Democrat gains, did little to change the partisan makeup of these state legislatures.

## THE CONTEXT OF KEY STATE LEGISLATIVE RACES

While many Americans cannot name the vice president of the United States, fewer can identify their state legislator. Further, many voters do not know the difference between a US senator and a state senator. Although constituents cannot recall the name of their member of Congress, they usually are able to recognize their name (Hinckley 1980). The success rate for recognizing state legislators cannot be much better. Combine this with the fact that there is little media coverage of state legislators, and the difficulty of running a state legislative campaign becomes apparent (Cooper 2002). Many state legislators often tell stories of campaigning door to door only to have constituents attempt to reference their work in Washington. These candidates often smile and nod rather than risk insulting the voter by correcting them.

This mistaken identity belies transferability between political issues on the national and state political scenes. Candidates and political operatives understand this and so will often create a state and local strategy that is built around a national campaign issue. It is a much easier strategy to construct than to educate the public on state public policy issues that they may know far less about when compared to national issues.

Each state has its own political processes and traditions, which can seem foreign to a voter from the state next door. This can begin to explain why a national electoral wave favoring one party spills over to some state legislatures, but not others. On the one hand, eight state chambers flipped on Election Night 2014, including both of Nevada's chambers. However, the only two states with split partisan control heading into Election Night, Iowa and Kentucky, remained in split partisan control the following morning. In this era of increasing partisan polarization, the GOP wave reached some states, but not others (see fig. 2.3)

Historically speaking, the state legislature that seemed to swing the most in 2014 was West Virginia. Both chambers flipped dramatically to Republican (albeit the Senate had help from a floor crosser) with swings rarely seen in Western politics outside of parliamentary systems. Yet, next door in Kentucky, the State House remained in Democratic Party hands. What made the difference?

In West Virginia, Republicans gained a net swing of seven seats in the West Virginia State Senate, tying the chamber at seventeen seats for each party on Election Night, only to have a Democratic member cross the aisle the next day, giving Republicans outright control. The State House was fairly close going into the election, 53–47 in favor of the Democrats. The Republicans managed to pick up a net of seventeen seats, giving the GOP a new 64–36 majority in the lower chamber. This is the first time Republicans have control of the West Virginia State House since the Great Depression.

Meanwhile, in neighboring Kentucky, many national and statewide Republican groups were focused in flipping the State House to Republican. The Democrats had a 54–46 advantage in the Bluegrass State while the Senate was stalwart Republican territory. Kentucky also had a fair amount of the national spotlight in 2014. US Senate Majority Leader Mitch McConnell was targeted by both Tea Party Republicans in a primary, while Democrats managed to get their strongest candidate into the race, Kentucky Secretary of State Alison Lundergan Grimes. The race

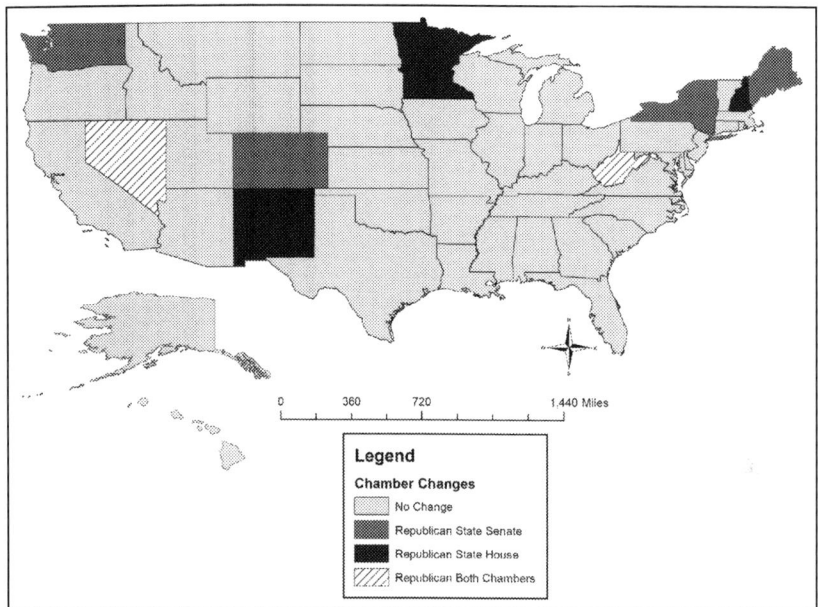

Figure 2.3. State Chamber Partisan Changes

cost close to $80 million, more than enough ad buys to carry over into down-ticket races. Yet, unlike other states in 2014, that was not always the case in Kentucky.

The State Senate had a Republican majority that expanded from 23–14 with one Independent before the election to a 26–12 result on Election Night. Meanwhile, the State House, held by Democrats, did not budge. The fifty-four seats out of one hundred they held before Election Night were exactly what they ended up with after Election Night. The difference in the results for the neighboring states is mostly due to two key factors.

First, the incumbent advantage is even greater in Kentucky due to the early candidate filing deadline. Candidates running under either party's political banner had to file for office by January 28, making it difficult for even the cagiest political opportunist to measure whether a November wave was going to materialize in the depths of the previous winter. This led to Kentucky having fewer competitive races: forty-nine of the one hundred Kentucky State House races had no major political party opponent. In stark contrast, only one out of seventeen West Virginia Senate races did not feature a candidate from both political parties. In the West Virginia House, it was nine out of one hundred. More races across the state, competitive or not, allowed more chances for West Virginia Republicans to catch the national wave, or rather, less chances for Kentucky Republicans to do so. Part of this is due to West Virginia's unique residency and election system in place for their legislative districts. One hundred delegates are elected from sixty-seven districts; each district elects anywhere from one to five delegates. In the Senate, thirty-four senators are elected from seventeen districts, two senators apiece. However, if a West Virginia State Senate district has more than one county, then that district's two senators may not come from the same county. As convoluted as this system can be when compared to a single-member district, the theme is clear. Larger districts that would elect multiple members encouraged more candidates to get in the race. The 51st Delegate district elects five members. It had fourteen candidates from the two major parties running in the primary for those five seats.

A second difference between Kentucky and West Virginia state legislative races was the backdrop of the federal campaigns. While Kentucky had its blockbuster US Senate race, none of its six congressional districts were competitive. However, West Virginia had an open Senate seat that switched from Democrat to Republican. Of the state's three congressional seats, one was open, and another flipped from Democrat to Republican. Despite the dollars spent by national parties being smaller than what was spent in Kentucky, the average West Virginia voter actually had more competitive up-ticket races, which may have made it easier for the wave to reach the mid-ticket state legislative races.

The only state to see both chambers flip party control as a direct result of the voters in 2014 was Nevada. Nevada is not only notable for its dual chamber flip, but also extraordinary because of the extent of the seat swing. In the State Assembly, the Democrats held a 26–15 seat advantage before Election Day, with one vacancy. This was reversed on Election Night as the Republicans would now enjoy a 27–15 advantage, a twelve-seat pickup for the GOP. Meanwhile, the Nevada State Senate flipped, but in this case only by the slimmest of margins. An 11–10 Democrat advantage became an 11–10 Republican advantage, which was erased in the 2016 election.

Similar to the Nevada Senate in the 2014 election, the Colorado Senate flipped to Republican because of a net gain of one seat. The old

18–17 margin for Democrats is now the opposite. This chamber is unique among the ones we have looked at so far; it flipped, but not likely because of the national wave. A major news story in the state and across the country in 2013 was the recall elections triggered by passage of a new gun-control law in Colorado. This led to a number of recall efforts against incumbent state senators in 2013, including a successful recall of the sitting Senate president, a first in the state's history.

On the other hand, another chamber that flipped and is often susceptible to national waves is the New Hampshire House of Representatives. In the nation's largest state chamber, four hundred members represent roughly three thousand voters each. Like West Virginia, they run in districts that have different numbers of members elected. Some districts elected one representative while others elected as many as eleven. This means that if one party does a good job turning out their voters in just one multimember district, several seats swing. For example, "Hillsborough District #37" elects eleven members to the State House. With a general election ballot of eighteen candidates in this district, eleven Republicans and seven Democrats, voters elected Republicans in first through eleventh place.

The national conditions were ripe for the GOP on Election Night as more than one hundred seats were either left open by retiring incumbents or vacant. The GOP won 239 out of 400 seats on Election Night, up from the 179 they won in 2012. The New Hampshire House has been in line with national trends in recent cycles. The Democrats won a majority there in 2006, 2008, and 2012, while Republicans won control in 2010 and 2014.

At the same time as the Granite State gave Republicans back control of the enormous parliamentary body, the State Senate remained Republican, slightly increasing the GOP majority to a 14–10 margin. The state reelected Democrats for governor, US senator, and a congressional seat. However, the other congressional district did flip from Democrat to Republican. It stands to reason that while New Hampshire was undoubtedly impacted by the national trend, the wild swings seen in the State House had as much to do with their electoral system as it did the wider Republican wave.

Next door in Maine, the State Senate flipped to Republican while the Maine House of Representatives remained in Democratic Party hands, albeit with a smaller majority. The Maine Senate campaigns stand as another great example of how fielding as many candidates as possible, thereby limiting "free passes" to reelection for incumbents, can increase the odds of a takeover by the minority party. Only one out of the thirty-five Senate districts did not feature candidates from both major parties. The Democrats held a 19–15 majority, along with an Independent senator who supported the Democrats. On Election Night, with a newly minted redistricting plan, the Republicans picked up five net seats to hold a new 20–15 advantage. In the Maine State House, Republicans picked up seats, but did not flip control as the Democrats now had a 79–68 majority, with four Independents.

In Minnesota, the State House of Representatives changed hands from Democratic-Farmer-Labor (DFL) control to Republican control. This chamber has flipped much like the New Hampshire House has, with the DFL winning majorities in 2006, 2008, and 2012, while Republicans won them in 2010 and 2014. This is a classic case of the national mood impacting state legislative races. In 2012 the DFL won 73 out of 134 seats.

Our final state chamber that changed hands on Election Night 2014 might be the most complicated story to tell, that of the New York State Senate. While the Republican Party officially won outright control of the chamber on Election Night, they had held a measure of control over the chamber for years due to coalition agreements with disaffected members of the Democratic Senate Caucus. Republicans held 29 out of 63 seats before the 2014 cycle, and they were able to reach the magic number of 32 after Election Night.

To understand why this chamber flipped, statistical analysis is not as telling as a short history lesson. The recent history of the State Senate is nothing short of a soap opera. After years of Republican control, the Democrats won the Senate in 2008. However, in the summer of 2009, thirty Republicans joined with two Democrats to challenge for Senate leadership. When one of the Democrats backed out, the chamber deadlocked, and with no clear lieutenant governor to break the tie (David Patterson had just been elevated to governor after Eliot Spitzer's resignation), a period of time ensued where there was no clear leadership of the chamber. Eventually, Democrats set aside their differences and controlled the chamber until the 2010 elections when Republicans won back control.

In 2012 the Democrats appeared to have won a majority again, only to have Republicans broker a deal with dissident Democrats to control the chamber in a coalition. In the summer of 2014, the Democrats remaining in the coalition agreed to rejoin the Democratic Caucus after the 2014 election cycle, but by that point the Republicans had achieved their majority yet again, reaching thirty-two seats. The New York Senate has a political culture all its own and this most recent flip likely had little to do with the wider national GOP wave.

## CONSEQUENCES

The most apparent consequence of the 2014 state legislative elections is the historically large numbers of Republican state legislators being elected. Given that Republican state legislators make up over 55 percent of all state legislators, it is clear that they have outperformed in this area and, because state legislative districts do not align with precincts or counties, it is not possible to determine districts where a Republican state legislator performed better than a top-of-the-ticket office like governor, US senator, or even president. However, one way to examine Republican state legislative performance is to look at what percent of the state legislature is Republican versus what percent of the state voted for Romney in 2012.

Figure 2.4 shows a scatterplot with a fit line. The percent each state voted for Romney in the 2012 presidential election explains almost 76 percent of the variance of percent of the state legislature in each state that is Republican. The fit line also provides some other key findings. First, despite the large number of Republican state legislators, there are several states where the number of Republicans in the state legislature underperform the presidential vote. Two notable states where the percent of the state legislature is less than the Romney vote are Kentucky and West Virginia. There are also several states where the percentage of Republicans in the state legislature overperform the presidential vote. They cluster in the middle of the figure above the fit line. These states are extremely prominent in that the cluster contains almost all the key battleground states such as Ohio, Nevada, Virginia, Florida, Michigan, Wisconsin, New Hampshire, and Iowa.

The consequences of the 2014 state legislative elections, despite being a "side show" to the congressional and gubernatorial elections, are massive in their scope for public policy. Given the American federal system that allows states to exercise a great degree of autonomy and be "laboratories of democracy," there are a great deal of policy initiatives that can be accomplished in the states.

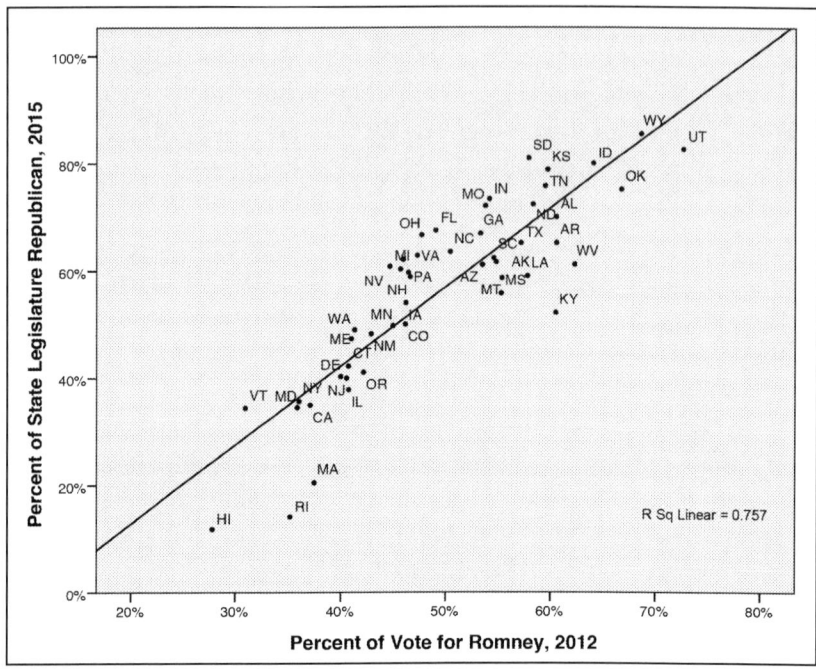

Figure 2.4. Scatterplot of Percent of State Legislature That Is Republican and Percent of Vote for Romney in 2012, by State

Since 2010 mostly Republican-controlled state legislatures have diligently targeted policy areas typically identified as being key issues for their base. The number of antiabortion laws passed in the states have increased dramatically since 2010 (Boonstra and Nash 2014). During this same time period, the number of laws relaxing regulations on gun ownership and the ability to carry firearms have also increased (Yourish, Andrews, Buchanan, and McLean 2013). Several Republican-controlled states have implemented voter-identification laws (Nelson 2014). Kansas' Republican governor and state legislature voted to decrease the income tax in the state. Despite criticism over lost revenue, the governor and state legislature vowed to continue the policy of cutting taxes in the state (Nelson 2014). Finally, several states in the Midwest have enacted right-to-work laws that diminish the power of labor unions (Davey 2015). In effect, many states have become laboratories of democracy for Republicans, and they are able to continue with their policy agendas.

Another ramification of the 2014 state legislative elections and the general trend of geographic polarization and sorting is that several state legislatures have veto-proof majorities. There is a growing number of states that have de facto legislative control because one party controls enough members in both chambers of the state legislature that they can effectively override a governor's veto with a party-line vote. Most of the states that have veto-proof legislatures typically only require a majority vote or a three-fifths vote as opposed to a two-thirds majority. Yet the number of veto-proof legislatures is still indicative of the growing entrenched partisanship in the states.

Finally, perhaps the most important consequence of the 2014 state legislative elections is that the unprecedented number of Republican state legislators provided a deep bench for future political races. According to the National Conference of State Legislatures, 44 current US senators and 215 current members of the House of Representatives are former state legislators (Hurley 2014). Two Republican candidates for US Senate who unseated incumbents in North Carolina and Iowa previously held office as state legislators. Former President Barack Obama is among several presidents who got their start in politics as state legislators (Hurley 2014).

## CONCLUSION

The 2014 state legislative election saw Republicans make unprecedented gains across the country and resulted in an equally unprecedented number of seats and state legislatures controlled by the GOP. These victories, along with the Democrats' ability to hold traditionally "blue" states, have allowed most states to effectively become laboratories of democracy for the two major parties. Both parties, having the "trifecta" of control of the state legislature and governor's office, have and continue to pass partisan policy initiatives. Given the sheer number of state legislatures controlled by Republicans, the party has a deep well of potential candidates to draw from in future elections. Finally, given the results of the 2016 presidential election, it may take several election cycles for Democrats to undo Republican gains in state legislatures.

# Up Close & Personal

## State Level Races

# Chapter 3

# Florida's Second Congressional District
## A Blue Dot in a Field of Red

*Robert E. Crew, Jr., Alexandra G. Cockerham, and Edward James III*

In the 2014 elections in the United States, Democrats suffered substantial losses at all levels of government. The party lost a total of 9 US Senate seats, 14 seats in the US Congress, between 300 and 350 seats in state legislatures around the country,[1] and 2 governor positions. One of the few wins for the Democrats in this grim environment took place in Florida's Second Congressional District where first-time candidate Gwen Graham became one of only two Democrats in the nation to unseat an incumbent congressional Republican. This chapter describes the campaign carried out by Ms. Graham and tests several hypotheses explaining the outcome. In so doing, we are able to shed light on the differential effects of candidate campaign strategies versus "the hand you're dealt" on election results more generally.

### FLORIDA DISTRICT 2: THE STRATEGIC CONTEXT

Florida's Second Congressional District is composed of the entirety of twelve counties and parts of two others. These counties are stretched over the central and western portions of the Florida Panhandle and are viewed as the classic Old South, with "cotton fields, soft pine stands, catfish farms, large families, small towns with large churches" (Barone and Cohen 2004).

While voter registration favors the Democrats, many of these voters have long since left that party philosophically and regularly vote for Republican candidates. Indeed, as the campaign began, most of the nation's most prominent political analysts, Sabato's Crystal Ball, Fair Vote, and the Cook Political Report rated the district as a "likely" Republican district or as a "leaning Republican" district. This Republican lean had begun after a long period of Democratic dominance in the district when that party's blue dog incumbent lost his seat in the "wave" election of 2010. In that race a combination of a poor economy, unhappiness with President Obama, and some courageous votes on the incumbent's part for the Affordable Care Act and other legislation fraught with partisan implications produced a 12.2 percent victory for a first-time Republican candidate, Steve Southerland, a Tea Party–backed undertaker from Panama City, Florida. In the subsequent election in 2012, Southerland was reelected by 5 percent of the vote.

Despite these two consecutive victories by a Republican, the district remained on the Democratic Congressional Campaign Committee's "Red to Blue List," which identifies districts around the nation that Democrats have targeted to flip from Republican to Democratic control. There were, as of October 2012, 86,590 more registered Democrats in the district than Republicans, and Democratic Party activists held out hope that the "right" candidate could bring back some of these voters to their original home.

## CAMPAIGN FUNDAMENTALS: PARTISANSHIP, PRESIDENTIAL APPROVAL, AND THE ECONOMY

In political terms, the Second Congressional District is two districts in one. Leon County (Tallahassee) and its neighbor Gadsden County are home to a large black population, a large student population, and a large number of what passes for liberals in Florida. The rest of the district is populated by conservative white people who have a very different view of the role of government and of the political parties than do the citizens of Leon and Gadsden Counties. This is particularly true for Bay County

(Panama City), home to a large military population, and its neighbors in the west. Leon and Bay Counties contain 67 percent of the registered voters in the district. A majority of registered voters in Leon County are Democrat (53.0 percent) but in 2014 Bay County was 70.6 percent Republican and is the bedrock of Southerland's support. In 2012 he won 72.5 percent of the votes in the county and its vote made up nearly a third of his overall total (32.4 percent).

Working against Graham was the president's approval rating. Typically, a leading indicator of election outcomes, President Obama's national approval rating was historically low at this period in his term. While the Quinnipiac Poll of January 31, 2014, showed the president's rating in Florida as slightly higher than in the nation as a whole (42 percent to 40 percent), his standing with the public was a drag on the Democratic candidate. While there were no comparable data for the Second Congressional District, few questioned that the president was highly unpopular in Bay County and in most of the district outside of Leon, Gadsden, and perhaps Jefferson, Counties.

Preelection polls in Florida showed that the condition of the nation's and the state's economy was the most important issue in the election and Republican candidates in 2014 made this the focal point of their campaigns. Economic conditions in Florida as well as in the nation had improved during the 2013–14 time period and, under ordinary circumstances, this would bode well for the Democrats. Nevertheless, polls also showed that most Americans were not feeling the impact of the improving economy and Democrats could not decide whether to be upbeat or downbeat. In this context, it was not clear how the nature of the economy would affect the outcome of the race.

## CANDIDATE-RELATED CONDITIONS

Congressman Southerland won his first race for public office in 2010 at the height of the nation's economic crisis and in the throes of the contentious debate over President Obama's Affordable Care Act. During this campaign, and subsequently, he settled into a Tea Party style that consisted of strident attacks on anything he did not agree with, particularly the ACA. In Congress, he voted to continue the government shutdown with the most ideologically conservative members of the US House. He held a 90 percent rating from the American Conservative Union and his personal style left many people in his district with an image of an angry, uncompromising conservative ideologue.

As a threatened incumbent, Southerland was given high priority within the Republican Party and his campaign committee raised $1,036,887 by December 31, 2013. More importantly, external advocacy groups that were supportive of conservative causes committed to supporting his campaign and Americans for Prosperity spent $160,000 on his behalf before the end of April 2014. In short, the congressman had the money he needed to conduct an aggressive campaign and much of it came from groups who traditionally have taken on the role of demonizing the opposition.

Despite these assets, Southerland was described as among the most vulnerable incumbents in the nation and the Republican Congressional Campaign Committee named him to its Patriots Program, which was designed to assist threatened incumbents in their reelection bids. His vote in 2013 against ending the congressional shutdown and extending the debt ceiling threatened to trigger economic havoc and led to deep disgust with Congress in general and with Republican congressmen in particular.

Gwen Graham, on the other hand, had never run for nor held public office and thus had relatively low name recognition in the district. She was, however, the daughter of Florida political legend Bob Graham, who had retired from the US Senate in 2004 (he had also been governor of Florida between 1979 and 1987) with a reputation as a political moderate. She had access to a multitude of individuals and groups who had known and helped him during his terms in office. Her strategy was to capitalize on his reputation and assets and take them as her own.

There was also a relatively large and well-organized Women's Democratic Club in Bay County that was poised to work on Graham's behalf and that helped in her efforts to increase vote share in that Republican bastion. Also in Graham's favor was a strong African American presence in the Second District that made up about 20 percent of the vote. One county in the district, Gadsden, is the only majority minority county in Florida and Florida A&M University, in Tallahassee, is a historically black school with a liberal and politically active student body. Left-lean-

ing outside groups also quickly began to line up behind Graham and she
began the campaign with a sizable fundraising potential.

## CAMPAIGN STRATEGY

During the course of her campaign, Graham adopted several broad
strategies that we outline below.

### Positioning Strategy

In the 2012 presidential race, President Obama won more than 61
percent of the two-party vote in Leon County and 70.4 percent of that in
Gadsden, but lost District 2 by 5 points. Graham's analysis of this
outcome, and of the strategic context just described, convinced her that
victory would come by increasing vote share throughout the district
rather than focusing on the two most liberal counties, Leon and Gadsden.

To implement this strategy, Graham adopted the slogan "The North
Florida Way," and positioned herself as a candidate who had grown up
in the district and who reflected the unique set of values and way of life
in Florida's Panhandle, an area that was viewed as culturally and politically different from the remainder of the state. In her announcement
statement she said that she wanted to be "a different type of representative and to find common ground with Democrats and Republicans." She
criticized the polarized nature of the existing Congress and promised to
work across the aisle for the betterment of the entire legislative district.

### Message Sequencing Strategy

Political candidates use both positive and negative messages when
presenting themselves to voters and must decide the sequence in which
these alternatives will be used. Gwen Graham adopted the "classic" mes-
sage-sequencing strategy (Faucheux 2002, 53). As is reflected in her television ad campaign, she opened on a positive note and made no initial
efforts to attack her opponent. As Congressman Southerland and his
supporters began their efforts to discredit her, she responded with nega-
tive/comparative ads and ended the campaign on a positive note.

Graham announced her candidacy on April 2, 2013, and immediately
began to identify and meet with political and community leaders
throughout the district and to attend political and grassroots events in

the fourteen counties involved. Throughout this period she emphasized her independent, moderate views and her willingness to compromise in order to achieve goals for the Second District. On June 16, 2014, she opened her television campaign with spots entitled "The North Florida Way," which called for a new approach to the way Washington works with an emphasis on North Florida values. Southerland and his allies responded with ads entitled "Both," saying that North Florida families cannot trust Graham. "She claims to be an independent voice, but has taken thousands of dollars from Nancy Pelosi, worked for ultra-liberal Howard Dean," and supports Obamacare. Others said she had been handpicked by Nancy Pelosi to run for the congressional seat. As the campaign progressed, Graham responded with attacks on Southerland's support for the congressional shutdown and for his insensitivity to issues affecting women. As the campaign drew to a close, she was advertising on a "dual track" with both positive and negative messages.

### Timing and Intensity Strategy

Campaigns must also decide on the timing and intensity with which they will present their messages. Graham employed a modified "bookend" strategy in presenting her candidacy to the public (Faucheux 2002, 55). She began with a strong effort to build her name recognition and to persuade her most likely primary opponent, Al Lawson, to refrain from entering the race. She followed this up with a slow, steady campaign buildup that included strong fundraising and an extensive travel itinerary that included contacts with community groups and individuals located throughout the district. Her campaign ended with strong fundraising and a multifaceted media message that was broadcast in all areas of the district.

Beginning nearly two years ahead of Election Day, Graham initiated a systematic canvas of the entire district, identifying and meeting with local party officials, local business people, and local community elites. This was accomplished in the old-fashioned way by the candidate herself, slogging from county to county and meeting to meeting with small groups. A separate activity in this effort was a series of events dubbed "Grilling with the Grahams" that she hosted with her parents in many of the counties in the district. She combined this activity with an enormous effort to raise money for the campaign. In this part of the campaign, she benefited enormously from her father's contacts and from the efforts of the Democratic Congressional Campaign Committee, which had initially refused to endorse her. Her superiority in this arena was established in her first-quarter report ($1.4 million to $1.1 million for Southerland) and she became one of only ten nonincumbents in the nation to raise more than an incumbent in a congressional race (Clozel 2014). She ended the campaign at a high level of activity and a "ground game," direct mail and television and radio ads that reached voters throughout the district.

### Persuasion and Mobilization Strategy

Graham's efforts to identify and mobilize supporters proceeded in the "traditional" manner (Faucheux 2002). The campaign sought to enhance and reinforce the Democrats' natural base, to identify undecided and opposition "leaners," to persuade these voters to her side and to turn out her supporters in early voting and on Election Day. In pursuit of this strategy, the Graham campaign mounted one of the largest and most sophisticated ground games in Florida's congressional campaign history.

Adopting the model created by Obama for America in the 2008 presidential campaign, the Florida Democratic Party hired multiple field organizers for the campaign, each with a specific geographic area of focus, along with a field director and a number of regional field directors. It also hired paid canvassing staff that worked over 1,500 shifts. Their work was metric driven and targeted by precinct and at the microtargeting level. It utilized software from Florida's Democratic Party and information from its voter file, consumer data lists, and state party and Organizing for Action (OFA) volunteering history.

### THE OUTCOME AND AN EXPLANATION

The election returns showed (1) Graham winning the three Democratic counties in the eastern part of the district, (2) Southerland winning the remaining nine counties, but (3) Graham winning a larger vote share than the 2010 Democratic candidate in each of these counties and emerging the winner by a margin of 1.2 percent, 126,096 votes to 123,262 votes.

*Explaining the Vote*

The academic literature explaining the outcomes of electoral campaigns indicates that two factors affect these outcomes: campaign "fundamentals" and campaign activities. Successful campaigns usually argue that something about the manner in which they conducted their campaign—the brilliance of their strategies, "cagey" tactical maneuvers such as one the Graham campaign cited of preempting front row seats at a candidate debate, the numbers and quality of media advertisements, or the size and tenacity of their "ground games"—was responsible for the victory (Levinson et al. 2014). Campaign consultants and scholars also cite differences between candidates in the relative number of dollars raised and spent on the campaign and the advertising advantage at particular times during the campaign as reasons for victory (Sides and Vavrek 2013, chap. 7).

Students of campaigns also suggest that campaign outcomes are predetermined by "the hand you're dealt" (Sides and Vavrek 2013, 11)—that is, by a set of "fundamental" factors such as the condition of the economy, the partisan affiliations of the electorate, and a number of demographic characteristics that structure vote choice regardless of specific campaign activities. "If individuals who have already decided to vote (perhaps even before the campaign begins) are the same individuals exposed to campaign efforts, the observed campaign effects may actually be spurious" (Hillygus 2008, 50–68).

Here, we test the effects of both sets of influences on the Gwen Graham campaign by constructing models that include measures of the two elements of the theory. We estimate the effects of these variables on two measures of campaign success—change in voter turnout and share of the vote by Graham.

## CAMPAIGN FUNDAMENTALS

We begin by identifying three fundamental features of the county electorates that are thought to structure vote choice in District 2. These include the distribution of partisanship, educational attainment, and the nature of the economy during the election year. (The small number of counties in the district severely limits our degrees of freedom and requires us to utilize a limited number of "fundamental" variables.)

The nature of partisanship in an electoral district is typically the strongest predictor of electoral outcomes. Despite evidence that many Democrats in District 2 vote regularly for Republican candidates, the percentage of Democrats registered in each county is likely to have a positive effect on the Graham vote share.

Educational attainment is a strong predictor of citizen participation in general and in electoral participation in particular. Thus, we use this variable, measured as the percent of the population in each county holding no high school degree, as an indicator of campaign fundamentals.

Academic research about the impact of conditions in the economy on congressional election outcomes suggests that other factors may be more important (Sides and Vavreck 2013; McKenna and Han 2014). Nevertheless, the condition of the state's economy was the issue in the 2014 election in Florida that was said by Florida voters to be most important and it was thought to be important in the Graham-Southerland race. We subject this hypothesis to a test in Congressional District 2. The condition of the economy is measured by the change in unemployment in the election year. We anticipate that positive change in the economy will be positively associated with the dependent variables.

### CAMPAIGN EFFECTS

The Graham campaign argued that it put in place one of the largest and most effective ground campaigns in the 2014 electoral cycle. We employ three measures of campaign effort to test these assertions. They include the number of field offices opened in each county by Ms. Graham, the number of field organizers assigned to each segment of the district, and the number of doors knocked in each county by her campaign.

### FIELD OFFICES

A number of studies of field offices in 2008 found that such offices garnered votes for President Obama, perhaps enough to swing the outcomes in three states (Masket 2009). Joshua Darr and Matthew Levendusky (2013) show that campaigns behave strategically when allocating field offices and argue that having at least one field office increases *turnout* by approximately 0.4 percent and *vote-share* by approximately 1 percent, all else equal. John Sides and Lynn Vavreck have calculated that President Obama's *vote share* was about three-tenths of a point higher in counties where his campaign had one field office and six-tenths of a point higher in counties where Obama had two or more field offices (Sides and Vavreck 2013, chaps. 5–6). Based on these findings, we hypothesize that larger numbers of field offices in a county will produce both a greater vote share and a higher turnout.

## FIELD ORGANIZERS

Not all field offices are equal and those with larger staffs or that are better organized might be expected to produce better totals for the campaign than staffs that lack these characteristics (McKenna and Han 2014, chap. 5). While we know of no specific research on the effect of field organizers, we assume they will have a similar effect as field offices do. Thus, we also hypothesize that counties with larger numbers of field organizers will also produce larger turnout and vote shares for Ms. Graham.

## DOORS KNOCKED

Campaign managers and candidates alike believe in the value of face-to-face contact with voters and the Graham campaign mounted a substantial door-to-door effort to make these contacts. Existing research on the effects of such efforts is mixed. Some of the research indicates that personal contact is effective in increasing turnout, but not in influencing voter preferences and that repeat contacts are relatively ineffective (Kramer 1970). Nevertheless, experimental research has shown that contacting voters through door-to-door campaigns is an effective way to generate votes for a particular candidate. The strategy "does not work miracles, but canvassing one hundred registered voters at their doorstep will…generate seven additional votes" (Green and Gerber 2004, 19). We use data from the internal files of the Graham campaign to examine the effect of such activities.

Our hypothesis is that larger numbers of doors knocked will be positively associated with larger turnout and a greater vote share for Graham's campaign.

## MEDIA EXPENDITURES

Another hypothesis regarding the outcome of the race focuses on the differences between the two campaigns in fundraising and in ad expenditures. Sides and Vavreck argue that an advantage of three ads per capita on Election Day translates into almost an additional point of vote share (2013, 10). We are unable to test propositions regarding this variable in District 2, but have data that allow us to speak to the proposition in general.

Ms. Graham raised and spent more money (about $500,000) on the campaign than Mr. Southerland did and, in cooperation with her political allies, also bought more television ads during both the full campaign and in its last two days. Data from Kantor Media show that the Graham campaign and its allies spent $3,306,070 on television advertising during the final three months of the campaign and purchased 13,158 spots. During the same time period, Steve Southerland spent $3,429,900 on 12,306 spots, a deficit of .001 ads per capita compared to Graham, according to data provided by Kantar Media.[2] We are unable to analyze these data at the county level and therefore cannot test their relevance in our statistical model. Nevertheless, the difference between the two candidates on the number of ads aired per capita is negligible and is unlikely to have contributed very much to the margin in the outcome.

## RESEARCH DESIGN

In this analysis, we are interested in the effect of both campaign "fundamentals" and campaign activities on vote share and voter turnout. Therefore, we employ two dependent variables—Gwen Graham's vote share in each county and voter turnout across counties. Since both of our dependent variables are continuous, we conduct the analysis with ordinary least squares regression.

The independent variables identified in the previous paragraph capture both campaign activities and campaign fundamentals in the twelve complete counties where Graham ran for office. Unfortunately, with twelve observations, our degrees of freedom are limited. Therefore, we were selective in operationalizing our theory. In order to test both the effects of campaign fundamentals and campaign activities, we included an indicator of each across all the models. Since all the campaign *activities* variables are highly correlated (i.e., the number of field organizers is related to the number of field offices and the number of doors knocked), we ran three different models for each dependent variable, each model containing a different indicator of campaign activities.

Each of the three models also contains an indicator representing the effect of campaign fundamentals. In the vote share models we use partisanship, in the turnout models we use education. In both models we also controlled separately for change in the economy. The inclusion of the economic variable to our analysis did not change our substantive findings nor did it have an effect on the dependent variables, so we therefore omitted it from the analysis. We use partisanship as our indicator for campaign fundamentals in the Graham vote share models since this variable has been shown to be an important predictor of a candidate's vote share. We use percent of the population with no high school education as the indicator of campaign fundamentals in the turnout models because the level of education in a jurisdiction is known to be an important predictor of turnout.

## RESULTS

The results of the model employed to test our hypotheses are depicted in table 3.1.

**Table 3.1.** OLS results for Graham Vote Share and Turnout

|  | Graham Vote Share Model 1 | Graham Vote Share Model 2 | Graham Vote Share Model 3 | Turnout Model 1 | Turnout Model 2 | Turnout Model 3 |
|---|---|---|---|---|---|---|
| Intercept | 8.39 (16.20) | 9.04 (13.41) | 7.00 (16.63) | 68.80*** (9.02) | 55.20*** (10.85 | 69.13*** (8.89) |
| Doors knocked | 0.03** (0.01 ) |  |  | -1.14 (0.85) |  |  |
| Field offices |  | 11.29*** (3.46) |  |  | 1.31 (2.93) |  |
| Field organizers |  |  | 3.52** (1.53) |  |  | -1.23 (0.88) |
| % Dem | 0.52* (0.26) | 0.44* (0.21) | 0.49* (0.25) |  |  |  |
| % no high school |  |  |  | -0.49 (0.41) | 0.09 (0.46) | -0.44 (0.38) |
| $R^2$ | 0.4415 | 0.5885 | 0.4340 | 0.1706 | 0.02786 | 0.1852 |
| Adjusted $R^2$ | 0.3174 | 0.4970 | 0.3082 | -0.0137 | -0.1882 | 0.0042 |

Significant codes: '***' 0.01 '**' 0.05 '*' 0.1

Voter *turnout* in the 2014 election in the second district was unaffected by any of the variables in the model. In this election, turnout was down by nineteen points from the preceding presidential year, and down 0.70 percent from the off-year election of 2010. Apparently, the electorate was reduced to participants whose individual characteristics drove them to vote regardless of campaign activities. However, the measure of the campaign fundamentals we used in the model did not capture these characteristics. Furthermore, none of the activities of the campaign had an impact on turnout.

Vote *share* was affected by both campaign "fundamentals" and the activities of the campaign. We explore the relationships involved in three separate models in which we isolate the effect of each of the campaign effects variables (field offices, field organizers, and doors knocked) when controlling for the campaign fundamental (i.e., percent Democratic voter registration). As expected, the number of registered Democrats in each county was correlated with the Graham vote share. Each additional Democrat in a county increased Ms. Graham's vote share between .44 percent and .52 percent.

All three of the indicators of campaign efforts have a statistically significant effect on Graham's vote share. For every 100 doors knocked, Graham's vote share increased by 0.03 percent. While substantively small, consider a typical campaign that hires 100 volunteers. If each of these volunteers converts or mobilizes 100 voters over the course of the entire campaign, it would result in 300 additional votes for Graham. In a county such as Jefferson where Graham's margin of victory was about 5 percent, efforts such as these might have produced a different result. For every additional field office opened, Graham's vote share increased by 11.29 percent and for every additional field organizer put into the field, Graham's vote share increased by 3.52 percent.

First Differences include:

1.  A shift in the number of *doors knocked* from the 25th percentile (450) to the 75th percentile (10,000) yields an increase of 3.03 percent in Gwen Graham's expected vote share [95% CI: 0.46, 5.57].

2.  A shift in the number of *field offices* from the minimum (0) to the maximum (3) yields an increase of 33.84 percent in Gwen Graham's expected vote share [95% CI: 13.35, 54.19].

3. A shift in the number of *field organizers* from the 25th percentile (1) to the 75th percentile (3) yields an increase of 7.056 percent in Gwen Graham's expected vote share [95% CI: 1.34, 12.98].

## CONCLUSIONS

This chapter addressed a number of factors that affected the outcome of the Graham/Southerland congressional race. Given the nature of our data, these conclusions must be stated as tentative and must be evaluated with a larger data set. Nevertheless, most align with previous research on this topic. The voter turnout in the election seemed immune to campaign activities and also, at least in the manner in which we measured them, to the effects of particular social and demographic characteristics in the district. This finding is consistent with other research that shows off-year elections to be peculiarly unaffected by political campaigns and by many of the variables used to operationalize campaign fundamentals (Sides and Vavreck 2013). The condition of the economy appeared to have had no bearing on the outcome of the race. This finding is also consistent with other research on congressional campaigns (Erickson 1990).

While Democrats in the district may not be as solidly committed to their party's candidate as they have been in the past, the number of Democrats in a county is nevertheless positively related to the vote choice for Graham. This finding should come as no surprise and is consistent with a line of research that stretches back to the first empirically based analyses of political campaigns. The size and nature of the Graham ground game had a sizable positive benefit on vote choice. In those counties where the Graham campaign opened field offices, placed more field organizers, and knocked on more doors, her vote share was improved. These findings align with existing scholarship on the effect of ground-game activities (Masket 2009).

The findings regarding the positive impact of the campaign activities are limited by the absence of information regarding the likelihood that any individual contacted by the campaign may have been inclined to vote for Graham and may, therefore, have been unaffected by the contact. In short, the relationship shown between campaign effects and vote choice may have been spurious and should be examined with individual level data.

## NOTES

1. "Republican Wave Capsizes Democrats," National Conference of State Legislatures, last modified November 3, 2014, http://www.ncsl.org/blog/2014/11/06/republican-wave-capsizes-democrats.aspx.

2. http://kantarmedia.us/product/cmag-advertising-data-reports-ad-alerts, accessed December 7, 2015.

# Chapter 4

# Not Set in Stone
## Nationalization and the Changing Face of South Dakota Politics
*Emily O. Wanless*

> *I am not on the ballot this fall. Michelle's pretty happy about that. But,*
> *make no mistake: these policies are on the ballot, every single one of them.*
> *—Barack Obama*

In a speech at Northwestern University on October 2, 2014, President Obama articulated what everyone already knew: the 2014 Midterm Elections were a referendum on his administration and its policy output. Pundits expected what is expected every midterm election when the president's office is not up for election. The in-party Democrats should keep politics local, embracing candidate-centered campaigns and the personal vote. Out-party Republicans, however, would focus campaign efforts not on their individual candidates or specific state issues, but on President Obama and Senate Majority Leader Harry Reid, the Affordable Care Act, and immigration reform.

This expectation surrounding a nationalized election narrative for Republicans is a result of a growing trend in congressional races, where election outcomes are increasingly tied to national politics. Scholars have noted a number of ways that election outcomes are increasingly determined by voters' mood toward the current political regime in Washington, but they have yet to study the nationalization from a campaign perspective. Case studies, such as the 2014 South Dakota Senate Election, are a natural vehicle for studying how campaigns nationalize, as they can provide rich understanding of the strategies employed. In early October, a single SurveyUSA poll prompted a massive overhaul of a floundering Republican candidate's failing campaign strategy. Transforming before voters' eyes, the heavily favored but underperforming Mike Rounds refocused his localized approach to a much more nationalized strategy. Given its quirky political history, South Dakota is one of the last places where a nationalized approach should triumph over a localized strategy. However, through analysis of the changes to the role of outside forces, campaign finances, and the issue agenda, the 2014 South Dakota Senate Election demonstrates that nationalization is a strategy which resonates with voters.

## THE NATIONALIZATION OF US ELECTIONS

Nationalization of elections occurs when individual races focus on national issues (Azari 2014). This nationalized focus occurs when an electorate is more attuned to national conditions and results in uniformity of tone, focus, and theme in elections across the country (Ragsdale and Rusk 2011; Clagget, Flanigan, and Zingele 1984). When races nationalize, outcomes are more about evaluations of the incumbent president, national policies, and the functioning of Washington rather than individual candidates. If the incumbent is unpopular, out-party candidates will attempt to nationalize the election, while candidates of the in-party will localize, emphasizing their own candidacies and state-driven issue agenda (G. C. Jacobson 2009).

A nationalized strategy has a number of characteristics that transcend individual elections. First, candidates will run on a national platform (Abramowitz 2014; Azari 2014), only acknowledging national actors and policy. Second, shifts in party support swings parties back to equilibrium (G. C. Jacobson 2009). Nationalized elections will return the waves or surges made in previous elections that inflated party support in that state. Third, outside forces play a role in the campaign (Azari 2014). Funding comes from outside the state, stumpers are national figures, and the media takes an interest in the race's impact on the country as a whole.

Finally, this nationalized strategy is employed across the country and in elections at all levels of government (G. C. Jacobson 2009). The presence of these components in the 2014 races would indicate that the midterms were, in fact, nationalized.

What motivates a congressional candidate to nationalize their campaign? Nationalization resonates with voters. The "fundamentals" are the factors that have repeatedly explained electoral outcomes (G. C. Jacobson 2009). Fundamentals emphasize national level factors like presidential approval and evaluation of the economy. Scholars have noted the correlation between vote choice and presidential approval in Senate elections (J. Campbell and Sumners 1990), evaluations of the national economy (Carsey and Wright 1998), in midterm elections (Abramowitz 2014), and in open-seat contests (Koch 2000). Turnout itself is stimulated by presidential approval (Godbout 2013). Voters respond to increased partisan behavior in Congress (Koger and Lebo 2012) and disproportionately show interest in the president's actions relative to other political actors (Hopkins 2014). Ultimately, a result of nationalization is a decline in the number of split-ticket voters and cross-partisan districts (Arbour 2014).

This voting behavior holds especially true in midterm elections, where electoral outcomes are largely considered to be a national referendum on the party in power (Tufte 1975) or a result of voters using retrospective evaluations (Fiorina 1978, 1981). Specifically, midterms reflect the current terrain and climate (Goldstein and Dallek 2014). The terrain equates to the number of seats up for election and the partisan makeup of those seats, while the climate depicts the public mood. When the climate is unfavorable toward a political party, and that political party has more terrain at stake, we see massive swings in electoral support for the out-party. Coming into the 2014 Senate Election, several seats held by Democrats were housed in Republican-leaning states. This was especially troubling for Democrats, as President Obama's approval ratings were nowhere near 2008 levels when these senators last faced an election. Given the terrain and climate of 2014, Republicans across the country believed nationalizing the midterms would be the most successful strategy.

If the 2014 midterms were to nationalize, they would be following a recent trend. Abramowitz finds vote choice has increasingly been tied to presidential approval (2014). In 2012, 90 percent of voters who approved of

President Obama voted for their Democratic Senate candidate, while 82 percent disapproving voted for the Republican Senate candidate. Currently, only 7 percent of the electorate votes cross partisan and 76 percent of the Senate vote share is explained by the presidential vote share (Brookings Institution 2014).[1] A large reason for the correlation between senatorial and presidential vote shares is the increased awareness of the president. Eighty percent of survey respondents follow the president more closely than any political actor, compared to only 12 percent following their governor more closely (Hopkins 2014). Voters give all this attention to the president despite knowing that he has little impact on their daily lives.[2] Given the salience of the president's actions, and subsequent approval of those actions, it is no surprise that nationalizing elections is a successful strategy.

## NATIONALIZATION AND THE 2014 MIDTERM ELECTION

States that Republicans gained in 2014 were states that did not like President Obama and whose partisan makeup favored Republicans. Exit polls indicated that voters were motivated by partisanship, with 92 percent of Democrats and 94 percent of Republicans voting for their respective party's House candidates (Arbour 2014). The correlation between presidential and Senate vote share was the highest since 1956. As table 4.1 reports, in the nine states in which Republicans picked up a Senate seat, approval ratings for Obama were overwhelmingly unfavorable.

**Table 4.1.** States Picked up by Republicans in the 2014 Senate Election by Presidential Approval

| State | Pres. Approval | Dem. Advantage |
|---|---|---|
| AK | 35.3 | -9.7 |
| AR | 32.0 | -6.7 |
| CO | 42.2 | 1.3 |
| IA* | 37 | -2.3 |
| LA | 39.4 | -0.5 |
| MT* | 30.2 | -17.7 |
| NC | 41.6 | 1.4 |
| SD* | 32.2 | -18.4 |
| WV* | 22.3 | 2.1 |
| Nat'l Avg. | 42.4 | 3.1 |

*Senate seat was an open seat race. Source: Gallup 2015*

Even at the state level, Republican candidates were disproportionately successful compared to Democrats. Eleven state legislatures changed party control to Republicans. The 2014 Midterm Elections led to more Republican governors than in the previous twenty years. Finally, the issues discussed across the country were uniformly about President Obama, his policies, and the dysfunction in Washington, DC. The Brookings Institution asked experts in the nine most competitive Senate races about the issues facing the campaign (2014). Table 4.2 indicates a nationalized election, with similar issues mentioned regardless of the contest or candidates. Five of the nine experts interviewed mentioned DC dysfunction as a major campaign theme, with three experts mentioning President Obama in particular. Six experts said that national issues were a central focus of Senate campaigns in their state, four specifically identifying Obamacare.[3] In Kentucky, the "national implications" surrounding Senator Mitch McConnell's election played a significant role in that contest. Pundits and scholars appear to be in agreement, the 2014 Midterm Elections was most certainly nationalized.

**Table 4.2.** Summary of Key Issues in Competitive Senate Races

| State | Issues |
|-------|--------|
| AK | Carpetbagging, **DC dysfunction**, **federal overreach** |
| AR | **Obama**, **DC dysfunction**, senior citizens issues |
| GA | Best candidate for job, **DC dysfunction**, jobs/ unemployment |
| IA | **Obamacare**, **economy**, abortion |
| KY | **Nat'l implications**, coal, **economy**, **immigration** |
| KS | **DC dysfunction**, 3rd party presence, *Citizens United/* campaign finance |
| LA | **Obama**, **Obamacare**, energy, **immigration**, **DC dysfunction** |
| NC | **Obama**, state Republicans, **Obamacare** |
| SD | EB-5 . . . recently **Obamacare**, Keystone pipeline |

*Source: Brooking Institution's 2014 Midterm Election Series*

The reasons for nationalizing races across the country in 2014 are clear. The incumbent president was largely unpopular, maintaining an average national approval rating of 42.4 percent in 2014 (Gallup 2015). The incumbent president's policies were largely unpopular. During the election year, 53 percent of those surveyed disapproved of the Affordable

Care Act, with an 11 percent increase among Independents who believed that the Affordable Care Act hurt them (Gallup 2015). The economy, another "fundamental," had approval from only 38 percent of Americans (Gallup 2015).

South Dakota's political climate was no different, and, as a result, all signs suggested a nationalized campaign strategy for Republican Mike Rounds. Additionally, South Dakota is predisposed to support a Republican candidate given its political landscape. Table 4.3 reports Gallup's annual "State of the States" for 2014, finding that South Dakota had the tenth lowest average presidential approval rating (32.2), the fourth largest Republican advantage in party affiliation (18.4), and the thirteenth largest conservative ideology advantage (Gallup 2015).[4]

**Table 4.3.** State Public Opinion Rankings

| Presidential Approval | | Party Affiliation | | Ideology | |
|---|---|---|---|---|---|
| State | % Approve | State | Republican Advantage | State | Conservative Advantage |
| WY | 19.3 | WY | 35.5 | MS | 36.0 |
| WV | 22.3 | UT | 33.1 | AL | 31.2 |
| ID | 25.1 | ID | 25.2 | WY | 28.8 |
| UT | 28.3 | SD | 18.4 | LA | 28.3 |
| OK | 30.0 | MT | 17.7 | ND | 27.5 |
| MT | 30.2 | AL | 14.1 | AR | 27.4 |
| ND | 30.9 | KS | 12.3 | UT | 27.2 |
| KY | 30.9 | TN | 11.3 | TN | 26.4 |
| AR | 32.0 | ND | 11.1 | ID | 25.3 |
| SD | 32.2 | NE | 10.9 | OK | 24.8 |
| National | 42.4 | National | -3.1 | National | 13.8 |

Source: *"2014 State of the States," Gallup*

Statewide, candidates practically assure victory by simply positioning an "R" next to their name. Coming into 2015, only one out of thirteen statewide positions was held by a Democrat and that was retiring Senator Tim Johnson. Out of the seven constitutional offices on the 2014 ballot, Democrats did not even field candidates for four of the offices. Coming into the election, 76 percent of the State House of Representatives and 80 percent of the State Senate was controlled by Republicans; 57.9 percent of the population voted for Republican presidential nominee Mitt Romney. Most problematic for any Democratic candidate in South Dakota are the dwindling party registration numbers. Since a registration high of 204,413 (38.5 percent of registered voters) in 2008, the number of South Dakotans identifying with the Democratic Party has decreased by 30,000 (a 5 percent decrease).[5]

The bleak terrain for any Democratic candidate, coupled with a national climate that favors Republican candidates, is not the only reason the Rounds campaign would likely employ a nationalized strategy. In December 2013 a scandal broke surrounding a federal visa program (EB-5) and alleged wrongdoings under Governor Rounds's administration. Rather than give this scandal more attention, the obvious strategy would look to minimize this local story and emphasize the Republican-favored national political climate.

## THE 2014 SOUTH DAKOTA SENATE RACE

Even with the signs overwhelmingly pointing to a nationalization approach, emphasizing local politics in South Dakota has largely been a successful strategy. Despite a disproportionate party membership, South Dakota has held a divided congressional delegation since 1957. Two of the most recent incumbent defeats, Senator Larry Pressler (R) in 1996 and then-Majority Leader Tom Daschle (D) in 2004, were attributed to the incumbents' nationalized approach and assistance from outside groups (Theiss-Smith and Braunstein 2005). South Dakota has also had a long tradition of "prairie politics," a form of retail politics that emphasizes the use of first names and unfettered personal access (Bart and Meader 2004). A survey of South Dakota voters found that at one point since taking office, approximately 60 percent of respondents had some sort of personal interaction with Senator John Thune (Lauck 2014).

An example of South Dakota's tradition of localized elections can be found in the two gubernatorial elections of Mike Rounds. Identified as "Smilin' Mike," Rounds won both elections with at least 57 percent of the vote and left office with a 62 percent approval rating (Montgomery 2014b). Reminding voters of his previous success in the announcement of his senatorial bid, Governor Rounds committed to maintaining this positive, localized campaign strategy: "I'm not changing my approach. I know there's more money involved in it and there's more outside groups that have an interest in it, but I'm going to do my best to maintain the integrity of a good, solid, appropriate race for people in South Dakota" (Montgomery 2014b).

The 2014 South Dakota Midterm Election featured a three-way contest for retiring Democratic Senator Tim Johnson's Senate seat. The partisan makeup of the state assumed the election would be a safe pickup for Republicans. The race had national implications because the seat's partisan switch was essential to Republicans' ability to take control of the Senate. However, its perception as a foregone conclusion kept the race out of the national spotlight until one SurveyUSA poll in October indicated a surprisingly tight race. The rise of a former senator's third-party candidacy, a local scandal, and an inefficient campaign strategy, offered a glimmer of hope for Democrats and gave cause for concern to national Republicans. A result of this new political climate was a wholesale change in the Rounds for Senate campaign strategy, shifting emphasis from past service and "South Dakota common sense" to President Obama and the dysfunction in Washington. As predicted, the race outcome was a lopsided victory for Republicans. However, the unusual path to victory taken by the Republican frontrunner is a fascinating case study for those who are interested in the role nationalization plays in modern-day congressional elections.

The contest started on November 29, 2012, when former two-term Republican governor Mike Rounds announced his candidacy, quickly becoming the frontrunner. Rounds's candidacy came with a tremendous amount of scare-off, a result of his significant statewide name recognition and extreme popularity upon leaving the governorship in early 2011.[6] Five months later, former senatorial candidate and current Sioux Falls businessman Rick Weiland emerged as the first Democratic candidate. Accounts of the announcement indicate that the statement was both shocking and rushed, as Weiland hoped to preempt former congresswoman and the national party's preferred candidate Stephanie Herseth-Sandlin from entering the race (Ellis 2014). Three-term Republican senator Larry Pressler announced his candidacy on December 26, 2013, indicating that his bid was about running the campaign he should have when he lost to Tom Daschle in 1996. He credits the loss to following outsiders' advice and strategy. His 2014 bid was to be a truly independent effort (Montgomery 2014a).

**Table 4.4.** Public Opinion Polls for the 2014 South Dakota Senate Election

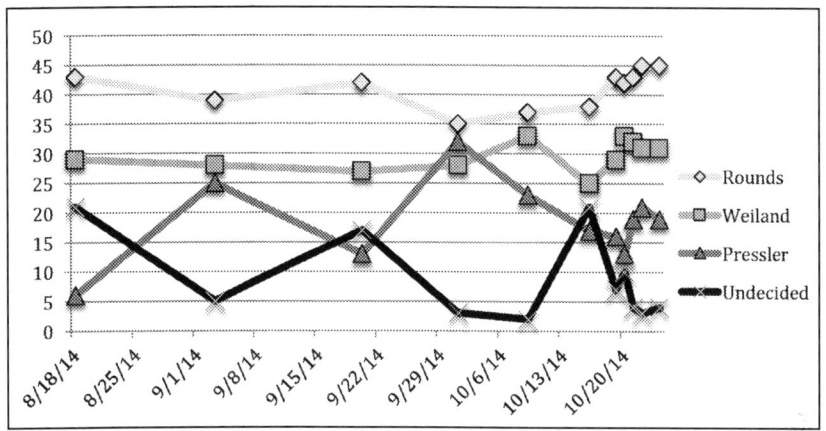

*Source: Real Clear Politics*

Table 4.4 reports all the major public opinion polls for the 2014 South Dakota Senate race. Initial polling indicated that Rounds started the contest with immense support from South Dakota voters. The first independent poll in May 2014 illustrated a campaign equilibrium indicating Republican victory, with Rounds leading Weiland by a twenty-point margin. The second independent poll indicated that the third-party candidate Larry Pressler was gaining traction. Throughout the summer and early fall, the Rounds campaign maintained their double-digit lead.

Throughout this period, the candidates maintained the status quo. The Rounds camp utilized a strategy similar to the one that won him the governorship twice. "Smilin' Mike" refused to go negative on opponents or nationalize the issue agenda, despite underperforming financially. His refusal to deviate from what was considered to be a proven campaign strategy at the state level generated grumbling from Republican operatives within the state and in DC (Montgomery 2014a). In contrast, Weiland, with little money and no national support, made the EB-5 controversy a major campaign theme, repeatedly associating the controversial investments for the visa program with the Rounds campaign. Because of Rounds's refusal to go negative, the Weiland campaign was able to dictate the narrative on the issue, implying that the corruption surrounding the program was a result of Rounds's mismanagement during his tenure as state executive. Initially, the Pressler candidacy gained no traction and had difficulty with fundraising; however, he slowly gained ground, largely taking support from Weiland-leaners and undecided voters (Tupper 2014). By September, he was polling within a few points of Weiland. The election's turning point was most certainly the release of an October Survey-USA/KOTA/KSFY/Aberdeen American News poll, where Rounds's double-digit lead was cut to a few points and Pressler led Weiland.

The poll triggered a wholesale change in the political environment of the election. Outside groups and national players began to take interest in this newly competitive race, donations now coming from national political action committees and the national parties. Strategically, Rounds finally went on the attack against his opponents, while Democrats were forced to decide whether to attack Rounds or Pressler, ultimately focusing primarily on the Rounds campaign. In the end, Rounds won the election by an even wider margin than expected (50.4 percent), Weiland reached his ceiling of Democratic support (29.5 percent), and Pressler underperformed when partisan voters returned to their base (17.1 percent).

## THE CHANGING FACE OF ROUNDS'S CAMPAIGN STRATEGY

Despite a crowded primary field, the former governor's initial strategy was to keep his campaign message about character, his "South Dakota common sense," and his success at running the state for eight years. Ignoring opponents' attack ads on the impropriety surrounding the EB-5 scandal, Governor Rounds refused to produce a single negative ad. Rounds utilized the same personnel and campaign tactics from his gubernatorial elections, touring the state on a bus, smiling, and reminding people he was a popular governor. Employing a local PR firm to produce his advertisements, the spots largely focused on constituent testimonials of his family background, values, and tenure as governor (Montgomery 2014b). Table 4.5 lists Rounds's ten advertisements produced for the primary and keywords describing the ad's message. Each of these ads featured actual South Dakotans or Governor Rounds. Content analysis of the ads finds almost no negativity. There is no mention of Democrats or his opponents, and only one mention of President Obama or his policies.

**Table 4.5.** Rounds for Senate Primary Election Advertisements

| Ad Name | Keywords |
|---|---|
| "Reacquainted" | Governor, family |
| "End Obamacare" | Obamacare, personal, SD, governor |
| "Ready to Work" | Knows SD |
| "Leader" | Experience, leader |
| "Pro-Business" | Businessman, governor |
| "Fiscal Conservative" | Experience, governor, budgets |
| "Approachable" | Knows SD |
| "Economic Development" | Governor, experience |
| "Values" | Personality |

Despite all the positivity and frontrunner status, Rounds's performance was considered to be underwhelming by many. His lackluster fundraising indicated a sense of complacency. The end of third-quarter fundraising for the Rounds campaign resulted in only $625,000 (Clozel 2014). To put this in perspective, similar candidates (open seat, largely uncompetitive, likely party switch) raised $1.1 million (Capito, R-WV) and $1 million (Daines, R-MT), respectively. Broadly, Republican political operatives saw the campaign as amateurish, naïve, and underwhelming. They implored the Rounds camp to give up on the localized tactics that had worked in his past gubernatorial contests (Ellis 2014). To observers it was clear: to win a Senate election a nationalized approach was needed, even in a state where *most* politics was still local.

A unique facet of this race was the campaign's transformation, which occurred right before everyone's eyes. What exactly changed? Almost immediately after the October 1 poll was released, campaign donations increased in size and stemmed from difference sources, an influx of national party surrogates speaking on behalf of Governor Rounds (Montgomery 2014a), and the narrative and tone of the campaign switched from an emphasis on Rounds and his ability to bring previous South Dakota experience to Washington, to President Obama, his policies, and the similarities both had to challenger Rick Weiland.

In terms of campaign finance, the post–October 1 poll period was vastly different from prepoll fundraising. Prior to the poll, outside donors were few and far between and donation amounts were meager. Table 4.6

lists all the PAC donations by committee name and date. Out of thirty-six donations, only four came before the October SurveyUSA poll: Every Voice Action PAC, National Right to Life PAC, and the National Republican Party's Victory Fund. The Every Voice Action and MayDay PACs both committed funding to Democrat Rick Weiland on October 6, and cut a series of attack ads associating Rounds with the EB-5 scandal. The Democratic Senatorial Campaign Committee, seeing an opportunity to disrupt a probable Republican gain in the Senate, pledged one million dollars for ad buys and field operations on October 8. In response, the National Republican Senate Committee (NRSC) entered the race on October 10, providing campaign funds, staffing, and new strategies.

**Table 4.6.** 2014 South Dakota Senate General Election PAC Donations

| Committee Name | Total Amount | For or Against | Date(s) |
|---|---|---|---|
| American Chemistry Council | $428,000 | For | 10/14 |
| American Hospital Assn. | $101,908 | For | 10/16 |
| Blue America PAC | $10,496 | Against | 11/2 |
| Credit Union Nat'l Assoc. | $62,000 | For | 10/22 |
| SD Dem. Party | $2,258 | Against | 10/9–10/11, 10/26 |
| DSCC | $388,238 | Against | 10/20, 10/24 |
| Every Voice Action | $995,002 | Against | 9/16, 9/18, 10/1–3, 11/13, 11/22 |
| Focus on the Family | $20,045 | For | 10/23 |
| Ind. Insurance Agents | $81,633 | For | 10/25 |
| Mayday PAC | $290,522 | Against | 10/22, 10/24, 10/29 |
| NRA | $1,047 | For | 10/25, 10/31 |
| Nat'l Rt. to Life (NRL) | $21,247 | For | 8/29, 10/6, 10/13, 10/17, 10/28 |
| NRP Victory Fund | $8,746 | For | 9/3, 10/28 |
| NRA Inst. for Leg. Action | $82,040 | For | 10/22, 10/24 |
| Progressive Kick | $101,350 | Against | 10/7–8, 10/15–16 |

*Source: Center for Responsive Politics*

A result of the race's perceived competitiveness was an influx of national party surrogates stumping on behalf of Mike Rounds. On October 17, Rounds campaigned with former presidential contender and national media pundit Mike Huckabee. He met with former governor, senator, and Agriculture Secretary Mike Johanns on October 29. And on October 30, Governor Rounds toured Sioux Falls with 2012 Republican presidential nominee Mitt Romney and popular incumbent Senator John Thune. With every campaign stop, these surrogates reinvigorated unenthusiastic South Dakota Republicans by emphasizing a national message of taking back Washington and defeating President Obama.

Justified in part by the large financial donation, national Republican operatives also undertook a more active role in the campaign. Despite offering up assistance and strategy as early as the primary season, the Thune camp and NRSC were largely ignored. After the poll, media members recount no longer speaking with Rounds's staffers; rather, they were directed toward Senator Thune's staff (Ellis 2014). The NRSC was now included in campaign strategy sessions. In total, ten national operatives from the NRSC and Thune camp, operatives with two successful South Dakota senatorial campaigns of national importance under their belt, were now making most of the campaign decisions (Montgomery 2014a).

One of the most dramatic changes resulting from the presence of national party operatives was a nationalized campaign narrative and negative tone. If you recall table 4.2, identifying the major issues in each of the major national races, South Dakota's was "EB-5 . . . recently Obamacare, Keystone Pipeline." Prior to the poll, the biggest issue for the campaigns was Rounds's involvement in a local scandal. However, after the SurveyUSA poll, the biggest issue was the Obama Administration. Table 4.7 lists the thirteen campaign advertisements made by the Rounds campaign for the general election, divided pre– and post–October 1 poll. Content analysis of these ads highlights perfectly how the campaign sought to nationalize their campaign mid-race. Prior to the poll, the ads continued the primary's message of previous experience, using "South Dakota common sense," and the personal story of Mike Rounds. Visually, these ads still utilized constituents and Governor Rounds's narration. Postpoll ad spots tied Weiland and Pressler to Obama and his administration's contentious policies, such as Obamacare and immigration. These ads had almost no mention of Rounds, and largely depicted images of Obama, Weiland, and Pressler, coupled with sinister narration.

**Table 4.7.** Rounds for Senate General Election Advertisements

| General election, prepoll | |
|---|---|
| "#ShameOnRick" | EB-5, attack |
| "Mike Rounds on the Issues" | Obama, Medicare, Obamacare, spending, Keystone Pipeline, SD common sense |
| "Work Effort" | Childhood, normal |
| "Here They Go Again" | Negative ads, EB-5, outside interest |
| "That's All They've Got" | Medicare, Obamacare, Keystone Pipeline, DC dysfunction |
| **General election, postpoll** | |
| "The Truth" | EB-5, dirty politics |
| "Our Values & Guns" | Weiland, Pressler, Obama, Obamacare, taxes, NRA, gun rights |
| "Our Values & Keystone" | Weiland, Pressler, Obama, Obamacare, taxes, Keystone Pipeline, Economy |
| "Thune Supports Rounds" | Thune, Obama |
| "You Would" | Weiland, Obama, Obamacare, big government |
| "Standing" | Ellsworth, economy, Thune, armed services, defense |
| "Keystone" | Values, tax increases, gun rights, Obamacare |
| "Ellsworth" | Values, tax increases, gun rights, Ellsworth Air Force Base, Obamacare |

Table 4.8 displays topics addressed in Rounds's campaign advertisements, dividing them by time period and frequency. Content analysis of Rounds's general election campaign ads finds a stark contrast between the themes of the pre- and postpoll ads. Ninety-one percent of the mentions of Obama and 75 percent of Obamacare references came in ads airing after October 8. One ad was entirely an endorsement of Rounds by Senator John Thune, insinuating that a Rounds victory would help take Washington back. However, themes prior to the poll were significantly more localized, with 73 percent of references to Rounds as the former governor and 80 percent of the phrase "South Dakota common-sense" occurring in prepoll ads. The local scandal surrounding Rounds was primarily discussed prior to the October 1 poll, with 88 percent of the references to EB-5 made in these ads.

The policy emphasis of the advertisements differed temporally. In the ads airing prior to the poll, the main issues discussed were local issues like energy, spending, and ethanol. The issues highlighted in the ads after the October 1 poll fundamentally changed, focusing on Obamacare, gun rights, Ellsworth Air Force Base, and taxes. With the exception of Ells-worth, these are largely national issues discussed in campaigns across the country. The tone of the Rounds campaign also changed. Only 5 percent of mentions made about his two general election opponents were made prior to the October 1 poll. However, Governor Rounds finally went on the attack, addressing the EB-5 scandal and comparing both Weiland and Pressler to President Obama and his controversial policies. If the voters took anything away from the postpoll set of commercials, it was that the 2014 Senate Election was no longer about bringing South Dakota values to Washington. Rather, the race was completely about defeating President Obama, his policies, and Democrats in Washington.

**Table 4.8.** Content Analysis of Rounds General Election Advertisements by Issue and Pre– versus Post–October 1 poll

| Mentions before October 1 Poll | Issue Mentioned | Mentions after October 1 Poll |
|---|---|---|
| 1 | Weiland | 13 |
| 0 | Pressler | 6 |
| 1 | Obama | 10 |
| 1 | Thune | 3 |
| 8 | Gubernatorial Experience | 3 |
| 12 | Washington Dysfunction vs. SD Commonsense | 3 |
| 2 | Obamacare | 6 |
| 2 | Spending/Budget | 0 |
| 1 | Economy/Jobs | 0 |
| 1 | Energy | 0 |
| 0 | Ellsworth | 4 |
| 2 | Keystone Pipeline | 2 |
| 1 | Ethanol | 0 |
| 1 | Gun Rights | 3 |
| 0 | Taxes | 4 |
| 7 | EB-5 | 1 |

## DISCUSSION

In 2014 pundits expected Democrats to keep politics local. Out-party Republicans, however, would focus campaign efforts not on their indi-vidual candidates or specific state issues, but on national actors and policies. The expectation that these races would take on a national tone stemmed from a growing trend of nationalized federal and state midterm elections. However, South Dakota has a significant history of keeping its politics local, and for Republican frontrunner Rounds this seemed like a good strategy to maintain given his success in two previous gubernatorial bids.

However, when an early October poll indicated the localized strategy was failing, a massive nationalization of the campaign ensued. The size and source of campaign donations increased and came from outside the state. National surrogates infiltrated the state to stump on Rounds's behalf. Campaign staff relinquished decision making to national operatives. And the issue agenda wholesale changed to comport with the expected nationalized narrative. The switch from a localized approach to a nationalized strategy worked, as Rounds rebounded to win the election he always should have.

Our understanding of the nationalization of elections can be improved with this case study from the 2014 Midterm Elections. While most races nationalize or localize from the start, the 2014 South Dakota Senate race provides the rare opportunity to observe a blatant switch in strategy. Given the success nationalizing had in South Dakota, a state least amenable to nationalization tactics, we can draw conclusions about the merits of using such an approach moving forward. Most notably, it appears to be a strategy that works.

We are also left with a number of additional questions to be explored in future research. First, which strategy used to nationalize a race resonates most with voters? Do outside forces need to have a presence, or is it simply the campaign's ability to nationalize the issue agenda that yields success? Second, are certain areas of a campaign easier to nationalize than others? Combined together, is a campaign able to run a hybrid nationalized-localized campaign or must the campaign be one tactic or the other to be successful? Finally, is the fact that South Dakota, an area that has valued localized races longer than most, an indication that all midterm elections will be nationalized moving forward? This study seems to make the case that even when the political environment is in their favor, candidates who want to win must nationalize.

## NOTES

1. From 1950 to 1990, the norm was that only 23 percent of the Senate vote share could be explained by the presidential vote share.

2. Forty-six percent of respondents said the president had an impact on their daily lives, while 31 percent said governors had an impact.

3. National issues include the economy/jobs, immigration, and healthcare. In two states, experts stated the Keystone Pipeline/Energy. Because these issues played a larger role in the elections in Louisiana and South Dakota, they are considered state-specific concerns.

4. The national equivalents were 42.4 percent, -3.1 percent, and 13.8 percent, respectively.

5. All data on South Dakota elections were compiled from the Secretary of State's Office.

6. A Rasmussen poll found that Rounds left office with a 62 percent favorability rating, with only 37 percent of the respondents indicating disapproval. According to the secretary of state's website, the partisan makeup of the state for this election was 45 percent Republican, 37 percent Democrat, and 17 percent Independent.

# Chapter 5

# The 2014 Senate and 2012 Presidential Elections in North Carolina
## A Microgeographical Comparison

*Adam S. Myers*

On November 6, 2012, Republican Mitt Romney edged out Democrat Barack Obama in the high-stakes contest for North Carolina's electoral votes. The final count showed Romney winning North Carolina with 51.0 percent of the total vote for both major-party candidates. Two years later, on November 4, 2014, Republican challenger Thom Tillis narrowly defeated incumbent Democrat Kay Hagan in perhaps the most competitive Senate race of the 2014 cycle. With all votes counted, Tillis beat Hagan with 50.8 percent of the major-party vote total—a partisan outcome nearly identical to that of the 2012 presidential election in the state.

The strong similarity between the statewide results of the 2014 Senate and 2012 presidential races in North Carolina is surprising given the fact that turnout in midterm elections is far lower than in presidential elections, causing the composition of presidential-year and midterm-year electorates to differ in certain respects (Campbell 1966; Wolfinger, Rosenstone, and McIntosh 1981; Jackson 2000). This raises the question of whether substate voting patterns in the two elections were as alike as statewide results might suggest, or whether they were actually quite different and the statewide voting percentages only aligned by coincidence. In this chapter, through use of the exceptional data resources made available by the State of North Carolina, the microgeographical foundations behind the results of the 2014 Senate and 2012 presidential races in the state are examined. More specifically, electoral and demographic data for North Carolina's 2,692 voter tabulation districts (VTDs) are used to investigate patterns of vote choice and turnout for both races at the most fine-grained level of aggregation possible in American electoral studies.

This chapter yields a variety of interesting findings. First, though turnout for the 2014 Senate race was much lower than for the 2012 presidential race, a remarkable association exists between VTD-level voting patterns in these two elections. Thus, the fact that the 2014 and 2012 elections in North Carolina featured very different electorates had little effect on aggregate voting patterns in the state.

While Democratic Senator Kay Hagan's performance across VTDs in 2014 largely mirrored Obama's performance in 2012, Hagan did consistently outperform Obama by a slight amount. Given the close margins of both races, Hagan's improvement over Obama's voting percentages would probably have won her the election but for another factor: turnout. Though turnout declined between 2012 and 2014 across nearly all VTDs in North Carolina, it declined more in Democratic-leaning VTDs than in Republican-leaning ones. It was this turnout differential, rather than differences in aggregate voting patterns, that likely cost Hagan the election.

The chapter begins with an examination of variations in the results of the 2014 Senate race across VTDs, pointing to the influence of several demographic variables (especially race) in explaining microgeographical voting patterns in North Carolina. From there, the chapter proceeds to show how similar the microgeographical patterns of the 2014 Senate race were to those of the 2012 presidential race, while at the same time pointing out that Hagan did consistently (if only slightly) outperform Obama. After demonstrating that Democratic-leaning VTDs exhibited larger turnout decline between 2012 and 2014 than Republican-leaning VTDs, the analysis turns to modeling the demographic and geographical factors that explain variations in turnout decline. Here, results show that the most important variable in explaining patterns of turnout decline was not the racial composition of VTDs but rather their age composition. Further, rural residence is shown to be a potentially important and underexplored variable mitigating against turnout decline between presidential and midterm elections.

## MICROGEOGRAPHICAL PATTERNS IN THE RESULTS OF THE 2014 NORTH CAROLINA SENATE RACE

The analyses of this chapter begin by presenting figure 5.1, a map of North Carolina VTDs color-coded according to Kay Hagan's share of the two-party vote for US Senate in 2014. The map shows that Hagan performed best in the inner cores of the state's large metropolitan areas, including Charlotte and Raleigh-Durham, as well as in heavily black rural areas in the state's northeastern and southeastern corners. Tillis, on the other hand, made his strongest showings in the state's Piedmont region, which includes the exurban and rural areas outside Charlotte and Greensboro. The most competitive VTDs in the state were in its far western end as well as in coastal counties in its northeastern corner. Thus, the patterns found in the map suggest that geographical differences in the 2014 North Carolina Senate vote mostly reflect the divide between urban cores and exurban and rural areas that has come to typify electoral politics in twenty-first-century America.[1]

To get a better sense of how individual level demographic and place-based factors affected aggregate voting patterns across VTDs in the North Carolina Senate race, variables pertaining to the demographic composition of North Carolina VTDs from the North Carolina General Assembly's redistricting website were collected and analyzed.[2] These variables included the percentage of blacks, Hispanics, persons aged eighteen to forty, and persons aged over sixty-five among registered voters in each VTD. In addition, calculations were obtained of the percentage of residents within a VTD who live in rural areas by collecting data on urban populations across North Carolina Census block groups from the 2010 US Census website, and then associating Census block groups with

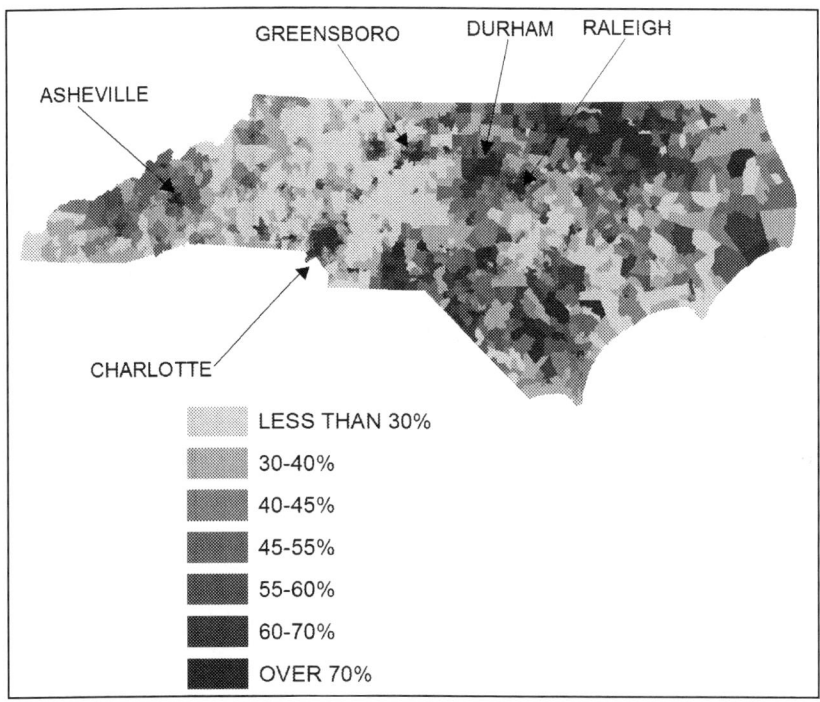

**Figure 5.1.** Hagan (D) Share of Two-Party Vote for US Senate, 2014

VTDs using ArcGIS. Because the resulting distribution of percent-urban across VTDs is bimodal (a very large percentage of VTDs are more than 90 percent urban or less than 10 percent urban, with few in the middle), a dummy variable was created ("rural") with a value of 1 for VTDs that are less than 10 percent urban and a value of 0 for all other VTDs.

Table 5.1 presents an OLS regression predicting Kay Hagan's share of the two-party vote for US Senate in 2014. The independent variables are the ones described in the paragraph above. All independent variable values were standardized by subtracting the mean value for the independent variable and then dividing by two standard deviations, as recommended by Gelman and Hill (2007) for multivariate analyses in which both continuous and binary predictors are included. Doing so allows for interpreting the regression coefficients on a "roughly common scale" (Gelman and Hill 2007, 56).

**Table 5.1.** OLS Regression Predicting Kay Hagan's Share of the Two-Party Vote in the 2014 North Carolina Senate Race

| Variable | Coefficient (SE) |
|---|---|
| (Intercept) | 49.0 (0.0)*** |
| Percent black (among registered voters) | 30.0 (0.0) *** |
| Percent under age 40 (among registered voters) | 13.7 (0.1) *** |
| Percent Hispanic (among registered voters) | 0.1 (0.5) |
| Percent over 65 (among registered voters) | 5.3 (0.6)*** |
| Rural (binary) | -6.1 (0.4)*** |
| n | 2,692 |
| $r^2$ | 0.73 |

*\* p<.05, \*\* p<.01, \*\*\* p<.001*
*All independent variable values were standardized by subtracting the mean value for the independent variable and then dividing by two standard deviations.*

Scanning table 5.1, it is clear that the percent-black variable is the principal workhorse among the independent variables included in the regression. An increase of two standard deviations in the percent-black variable results, on average, in an increase of 30 percent in Hagan's vote share. The percentage of registered voters under age forty is the next most influential variable, with an increase of two standard deviations in its value leading to a 13.7 percent increase in Hagan's vote share. Interestingly, the percentage of registered voters over sixty-five also registers a highly statistically significant, positive relationship with Hagan's vote share, though its influence is not as large. That the association here is positive may be related to the fact that older white southerners (i.e., those who came of age before the civil rights era) are more likely to have maintained their ancestral affiliation with the Democratic party than white southern baby boomers (McKee 2010).

Less surprising than the effect of the percentage of older voters is the effect of the dichotomous "rural" variable, whose coefficient demonstrates a statistically significant, negative relationship with Hagan's vote share. The significance of this coefficient suggests that Hagan's loss may be partially attributable to a poor performance in rural areas. Finally, the variable pertaining to the percentage of registered voters who are Hispanic registers a tiny and statistically insignificant coefficient, something that is unsurprising since Hispanics, for the moment, constitute a very small share of the North Carolina electorate, both across and within VTDs.

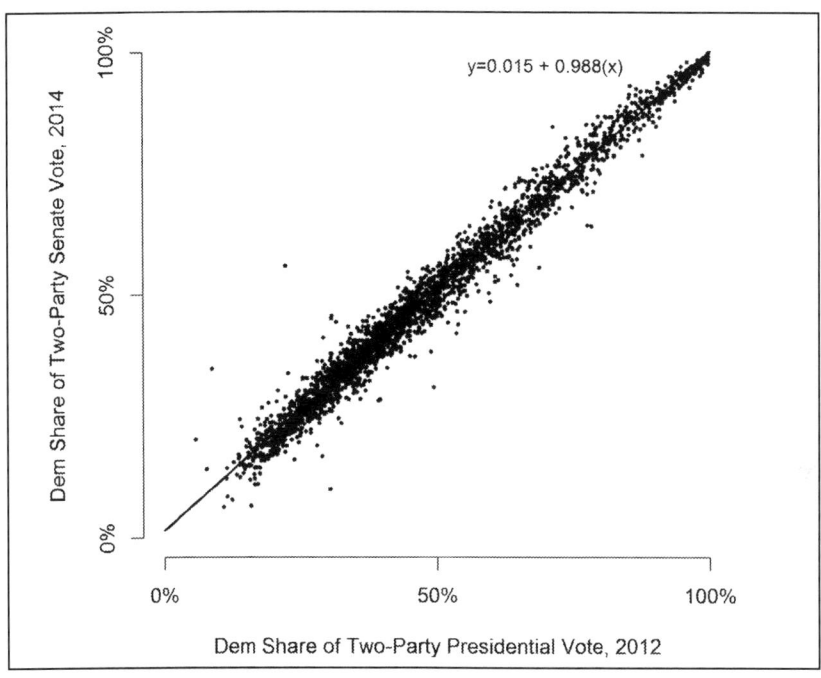

y=0.015 + 0.988(x)

**Figure 5.2.** A Comparison of the 2012 Presidential and 2014 Senate Results across NC VTDs

Taken as a whole, then, the results in table 5.1 show that Kay Hagan performed best in VTDs with large percentages of African Americans, younger voters, and (interestingly) older voters, while Thom Tillis racked up a large share of votes in overwhelmingly white VTDs and rural VTDs.

## THE STRIKING SIMILARITY BETWEEN AGGREGATE ELECTORAL PATTERNS IN 2014 AND 2012

If the map in figure 5.1 displayed Obama's share of the two-party presidential vote in 2012 rather than Hagan's share of the two-party Senate vote in 2014, or if table 5.1 exhibited the results of a regression predicting Obama's performance in 2012 rather than Hagan's in 2014, very little would be different because geographical patterns in the results of both elections were nearly identical. Figure 5.2 is a scatterplot comparing Obama's share of the two-party vote for president in 2012 (x-axis) with Hagan's share of the two-party vote in 2014 (y-axis), complete with a regression line. As can be seen, the scatterplot shows a relationship approaching perfect linearity (the correlation coefficient for the relationship is a staggering 0.988). The near-collinearity of the relationship between the results of these two elections is remarkable when one considers the dramatic difference in turnout rates for each. Whereas in 2012 over 4.5 million North Carolinians cast ballots for president, in 2014 less than 3 million cast ballots for US Senate. At the VTD level, the number of voters casting ballots in the 2014 Senate race was, on average, 65 percent of the number of voters casting ballots in the 2012 presidential race.

Given the fact that the 2012 presidential race and the 2014 Senate race featured electorates that were clearly quite different (in size if nothing else), how can it be that these differences resulted in almost no change in microgeographical voting patterns? Answering this question would require a highly detailed study of North Carolina's voter file that is well beyond the scope of this chapter. Part of the explanation is likely related to the ongoing process of microgeographical sorting that has become a well-known aspect of American electoral politics in recent decades. Stated simply, much evidence suggests that, since the 1980s, small-scale geographies in the United States have become more demographically and politically homogeneous and no longer contain the diverse mix of political groups they once did.[3] As microgeographical units in American politics become more politically homogeneous, it becomes less likely that differences in turnout levels within them will affect aggregate voting patterns. Thus, we should not expect that differences in turnout levels will affect electoral outcomes within VTDs very much. Instead, such differences are more likely to affect the influence of individual VTDs on the overall statewide election outcome (a topic to which I will return).

To be sure, aggregate voting patterns in the 2014 Senate race were not identical to those of 2012. The y-intercept of the regression line in figure 9.2 is 0.015, suggesting that, on average, Hagan did slightly better than Obama across VTDs. This is indeed the case, as Hagan outperformed Obama in 1,684 of the state's VTDs while Obama outperformed Hagan in only 965. Moreover, Hagan outperformed Obama by an average of 2.7 percent in the former, while Obama outperformed Hagan by an average of only 2.0 percent in the latter. Thus, while voting patterns in the two elections were extremely similar, Hagan did improve on Obama's perfor-

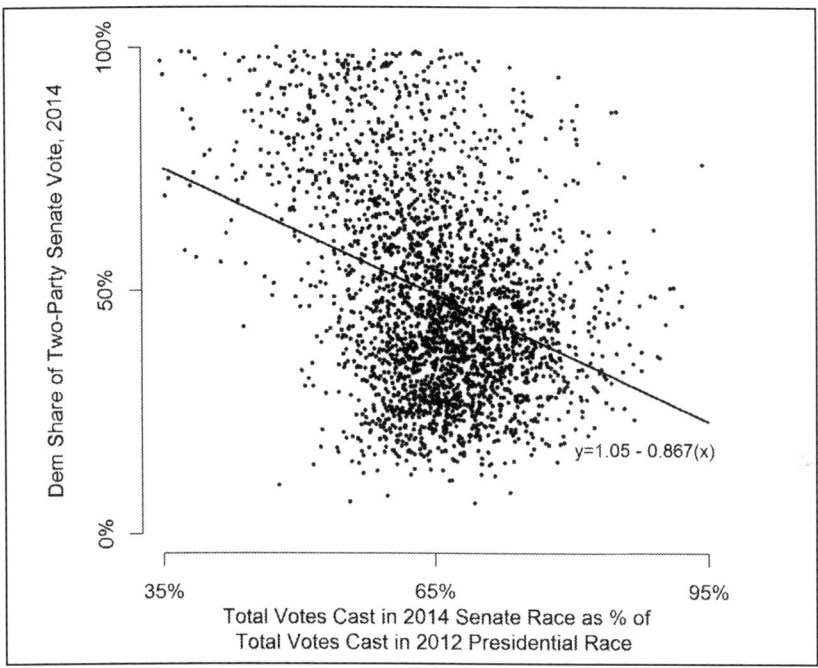

y=1.05 - 0.867(x)

**Figure 5.3.** The Relationship between 2012-2014 Turnout Decline and Democratic Strength across North Carolina VTDs

mance on the whole. In most elections such a minor improvement would not be significant, but Romney bested Obama with only 51 percent of the two-party vote share in North Carolina in 2012. Given the narrow margin between Obama and Romney in 2012, a minor improvement over Obama's performance on Hagan's part could potentially have allowed her to win.

Here, of course, is where the decline in turnout becomes a crucial matter. To say that the large differences in turnout for the 2014 and 2012 races did not appreciably affect aggregate voting patterns across VTDs in North Carolina is not to say that such differences were fairly even across the VTDs. They were not. While the number of voters who cast ballots declined between 2012 and 2014 in nearly every VTD in North Carolina, it declined much more in some VTDs than others. Figure 5.3 plots total votes cast in the 2014 Senate race as a percentage of total votes cast in the 2012 presidential race (x-axis) against Kay Hagan's share of the two-party vote in the 2014 Senate race (y-axis). A clear negative relationship exists, one that is mostly driven by VTDs near the top of the plot (i.e., those that supported Hagan overwhelmingly in 2014). These VTDs on average exhibited a significantly greater decline in total votes cast in the 2014 Senate race vis-à-vis the 2012 presidential race than others.

In order to gain a sense of whether the greater decline in turnout among Democratic (pro-Hagan) VTDs was pivotal in the outcome of the 2014 Senate election, I calculated what the statewide vote totals for Hagan and Tillis would have been had each candidate earned the same votes shares within VTDs but with the *total votes cast in each VTD at 2012 levels*. Under such a scenario, Hagan would have received 2,164,281 votes (48.2 percent of the total vote) while Tillis would have received 2,152,125 (47.9 percent of the popular vote). Thus, Hagan would have won. This scenario is, of course, based on the completely untenable assumption that 2014 vote shares would have been exactly the same had total votes cast been at 2012 levels. Nevertheless, as a simple exercise in considering whether differences in the extent of turnout decline across VTDs could have made the difference in the election outcome, it is instructive.

## EXPLAINING VARIATIONS IN TURNOUT DECLINE BETWEEN 2012 AND 2014 AMONG NORTH CAROLINA VTDS

The results of the previous section suggest that, given the extremely strong association between 2012 presidential and 2014 senatorial voting patterns across North Carolina VTDs, the higher decline in turnout among Democratic VTDs between 2012 and 2014 may have been crucial in delivering the 2014 Senate election to Thom Tillis. The question that this section seeks to address is, what factors explain why turnout decline was higher in some VTDs than others? Put differently, what demographic and geographic factors worked to benefit Tillis in terms of aggregate turnout patterns in the 2012 North Carolina Senate race?

The literature on turnout in American elections as well as data-driven accounts of the 2014 North Carolina Senate race in particular suggest that age and (to a lesser extent) race are likely to be important demographic factors explaining aggregate turnout decline. Michael McDonald (2010) points out that young people are more likely to vote in presidential elections and forego voting in midterm elections than any other age group. Examining the North Carolina voter file, Nate Cohn (2014) finds that North Carolina voters in 2014 were "distinctly whiter, older, and more Republican" than in 2012, but adds that most of the difference in the racial composition of the North Carolina electorate in 2012 can be attributed to lower youth turnout rather than lower black turnout (the black turnout rate, he points out, is not very different from the white turnout rate after taking age into account). Based on these accounts, the age and racial composition of North Carolina VTDs are clearly critical factors to include in an account of geographical variations in turnout in the state's 2014 Senate race.

Analyses of turnout based on individual level data like the ones discussed above tend to emphasize purely demographic factors like age or race, but it is also possible that place-based, contextual factors may impact turnout rates. In particular, rural VTDs in North Carolina may have experienced less turnout decline between 2012 and 2014 than nonrural VTDs. The impact of urban/rural location on turnout has not been well studied (the last article I found on the subject was published in 1977), but there are reasons to believe that turnout decline between presidential and midterm elections may be lower in rural areas than urban areas. First, rural Americans are more likely to be homeowners than other Americans, making them less mobile and more rooted in their communities than nonrural residents (Gimpel and Karnes 2005). Higher levels of rootedness may mean that rural residents have stronger relationships with local officeholders and feel a greater stake in down-ballot election outcomes, making their decision to vote less influenced by the pull of a high-profile presidential campaign. Second, because of their lower mobility levels, rural residents are less likely to need to reregister to vote or update their addresses with election authorities, and more likely to know where their polling places are located, making the voting process easier for them. Indeed, previous research suggests that the turnout differential between presidential and midterm elections is very high among recent relocators, precisely because midterm elections do not interest many Americans to such an extent that they are willing to overcome the barriers to voting in a new jurisdiction (Jackson 2000).

Table 5.2 presents an OLS regression predicting turnout decline between the 2012 presidential race and the 2014 Senate race across VTDs.

Turnout decline is calculated as follows:

$$100 * (1 - \frac{total\ votes\ cast\ in\ 2014\ senate\ race}{total\ votes\ cast\ in\ 2012\ presidential\ race})$$

Thus, a VTD in which the total number of votes cast in the 2014 Senate race was 76 percent of the total votes cast in the 2012 presidential race would receive a turnout decline value of 24 percent, while a VTD in which the total number of 2014 Senate votes was 42 percent of the total presidential votes would receive a turnout decline value of 58 percent. The independent variables are the same as the ones used in the regression predicting Hagan's vote share. Once again, all independent variable values were standardized by subtracting the mean value for each and then dividing by two standard deviations.

**Table 5.2.** OLS Regression Predicting Turnout Decline between 2012 and 2014 among North Carolina VTDs

| Variable | Coefficient (SE) |
|---|---|
| (Intercept) | 34.8 (0.1)*** |
| Percent black (among registered voters) | 4.9 (0.3)*** |
| Percent under age 40 (among registered voters) | 8.5 (0.4)*** |
| Percent Hispanic (among registered voters) | 1.8 (0.3)*** |
| Percent over 65 (among registered voters) | 0.5 (0.4) |
| Rural (binary) | -0.8 (0.3)** |
| n | 2,692 |
| $r^2$ | 0.46 |

*$p<.05$, ** $p<.01$, *** $p<.001$
*All independent variable values were standardized by subtracting the mean value for the independent variable and then dividing by two standard deviations.*

Unlike the regression featured in table 5.1, which shows that the percentage of black voters was by far the most important predictor of VTD-level election results, the regression featured in table 5.2 shows that percentage of younger voters is the most important predictor of VTD-level turnout decline. An increase of two standard deviations in the percentage of registered voters under forty years of age results, on average, in a decline of 8.5 percent in total votes cast in 2014 as a percentage of total votes cast in 2012. This relationship is highly statistically significant. The variables pertaining to the racial composition of North Carolina VTDs also produce a statistically significant decline in turnout, with percent-black unsurprisingly producing a larger effect than percent-Hispanic. Interestingly, the percentage of voters over age sixty-five in a VTD does not produce a statistically significant effect on turnout decline, meaning that VTDs with a high percentage of older voters do not exhibit meaningfully different rates of turnout change with all the other independent variables taken into account.

The most intriguing results in table 5.2 are those pertaining to the dichotomous "rural" variable. As the table shows, this variable produces a statistically significant negative coefficient, meaning that it is associated with *less* turnout decline. The size and significance of the rural variable demonstrates that rural VTDs exhibit meaningfully lower rates of turnout decline than nonrural VTDs even with all the other independent variables held constant. Thus, the evidence presented in table 5.1 provides some tentative support for the hypothesis that the "rootedness" of rural Americans causes turnout levels in rural areas to be less driven by the pull of a presidential election.

## CONCLUSION

This chapter examined why the final outcomes of the 2014 Senate race and the 2012 presidential race in North Carolina were so similar by delving deeply into the state's political geography. The exploration has unearthed a number of important and intriguing results. First, findings show that the principal reason for why the outcomes of the two elections were so similar is because the microgeographical patterns behind both outcomes were close to identical. In both elections, Democratic candidates performed most strongly in VTDs with large percentages of blacks and younger voters, while Republican candidates performed most strongly in predominantly white VTDs located in rural areas. The near-symmetry in voting patterns between the two elections is surprising considering that the total number of votes cast in each election was very different. While the cause of this symmetry amid such divergent turnout rates merits further study, one can speculate that it has to do with the microgeographical sorting of the American electorate. Such sorting has caused North Carolina VTDs to become more politically homogeneous, making it increasingly unlikely that changes in turnout across elections will result in electorates with fundamentally different political characteristics *within VTDs.*

Despite the near-symmetry in the 2014 and 2012 election results, the closeness of the margins in both elections suggests that, given Hagan's consistent outperformance of Obama across VTDs, she may have won the election had turnout rates *across* VTDs been the same as they had been in 2012. Indeed, the findings suggest that VTDs with higher shares of younger voters (and, less importantly, higher shares of black voters) exhibited higher rates of turnout decline than did other VTDs. It was the decline in turnout among these VTDs that likely cost Hagan the election. Findings also show that rural VTDs experienced less turnout decline than other VTDs, possibly because rural residents are less mobile and more rooted in their communities than nonrural residents. These findings reinforce Gimpel and Karnes's (2005) call for political scientists to more closely consider the ways in which rural political contexts are distinctive, in this case in the arena of turnout in midterm elections. The results of this chapter support and build on a number of previous findings in the political science literature concerning turnout differences between presidential and midterm elections. For example, prior work has shown that age is the most important individual level demographic characteristic affecting turnout across elections (see, e.g., Campbell 1966; Wolfinger, Rosenstone, and McIntosh 1981; Jackson 2000; and McDonald 2010), a finding that is consistent with this chapter's results showing that variations in turnout decline across North Carolina VTDs are best explained by the percentage of registered voters under the age of forty within a VTD. Prior work has also shown that turnout decline between presidential and midterm elections is higher among those who have recently relocated (Jackson 2000). This chapter has pointed to a previously unnoticed potential consequence of this relationship: differences in turnout between presidential and midterm elections tend to be greater in urban areas than in rural areas.

Beyond their significance for political science, this chapter's results also speak to important trends in American elections that are of interest to political practitioners and observers as well as academics. First, they point to the importance of a well-known and fundamental problem Democrats face in midterm elections in North Carolina and elsewhere, namely, that turnout rates within their geographical bases decline during midterms more than they do within the geographical bases of Republicans. The 2014 North Carolina Senate race provides an exceptionally clear example of a contest in which geographical differences in turnout decline between presidential and midterm elections may have made the difference in the final election outcome.

Lastly, this study's findings shed light on an important consequence of the geographical sorting of the American electorate: the stabilization of geographical voting patterns across elections. As American microgeographies become more politically homogeneous, the color patterns of American electoral maps are likely to look more or less the same in election after election... at least when those maps depict aggregate voting outcomes. When those maps depict patterns in *turnout*, on the other hand, they will undoubtedly look very different depending on the election at hand. Thus, turnout rates may well become the dependent variable most likely to interest political geographers in upcoming election years.

## NOTES

1. The state does contain certain "anomalies" in American political geography, the rural, majority-black counties in its northeastern corner being the most prominent example. For more about such anomalies, see Morrill et al. 2007.

2. http://www.ncleg.net/representation/Content/BaseData/BD2011.aspx, accessed March 12, 2015.

3. On microgeographical sorting in American politics, see, e.g., Bishop 2008; Myers 2013; Lang and Pearson-Merkowitz 2014; and Sussell and Thomson 2015. Scholars increasingly agree that a significant amount of microgeographical sorting (or geographical partisan sorting, as it is sometimes called) has occurred, though exactly how much is a subject for debate. For a contrary view on microgeographical sorting, see Abrams and Fiorina 2012.

Chapter 6

# Scott Brown and the "Carpetbagger" Label
## The Political Rhetoric Surrounding the US Senate Race in New Hampshire in 2014

*Jerome J. Day, Tauna S. Sisco, and Christopher J. Galdieri*

Few terms in the American political lexicon are more derogatory than "carpetbagger," and to be so labeled immediately throws a candidate off-balance. He or she is put on the defensive and must make common cause with would-be constituents in visceral ways. Big ideas, grand visions, technical details, and even big bucks, in and of themselves, do not defeat the poisonous hiss of "carpetbagger." This chapter analyzes the emergence of the carpetbagger rhetoric in a unique New England Senate race: former Republican Massachusetts' Senator Scott Brown who moved a few miles north and crossed state lines to run against incumbent New Hampshire Democrat, Senator Jeanne Shaheen. Using textual analysis, we analyze New Hampshire news sources' construction of Brown as a carpetbagger, a problematic sociohistorical trope in electoral politics, and the ways the carpetbagger trope was deployed and impacted his campaign. Finally, we assess what the carpetbagger issue might reveal about American politics generally.

## SCOTT BROWN: MASSACHUSETTS SENATOR TO NEW HAMPSHIRE SENATE CANDIDATE

Carpetbaggers are, in the public mind, opportunists, exploiters, and manipulators—claims made against politicians generally, of course, but, here, raised to the third power. The term originated in southern newspaper editorials during Reconstruction, as editors sought to create an all-purpose slur against northern whites who had moved south after the war and who were, with freed blacks, rewriting state constitutions under the Reconstruction Act of 1867. They settled on "carpetbagger" because it suggested rootless interlopers come south to exploit the defeated region, and could win the sympathy of northerners who thought there was something fundamentally unfair about southern states being represented by northern emigrants (Tunnell 2006). It should also be noted that many of those derided as carpetbaggers had in fact moved south in pursuit of business or farming opportunities several years before engaging in politics (Current 1967). But the reality of the situation could not counter the visceral negative reaction many—north and south alike—had to the idea of carpetbagging as a concept, and the term quickly spread beyond the South. Carpetbaggers have among the worst reputations in US politics, even though notable figures from Daniel Webster to Robert Kennedy have moved from one state to another to serve.

In 2010 Scott Brown defeated Attorney General Martha Coakley in a special election for the Senate seat vacated by the death of Edward Kennedy in August 2009. News agencies from Massachusetts lost no time in portraying him as a Republican David to the Goliath-like Democratic machine in the Bay State. With his 51.9 percent victory, Brown morphed "from an obscure state senator to a giant-killer in the Republican Party" (Viser and Estes 2010). Observers saw several factors at work in the Brown victory, but the Obama presidency cast a big shadow—or ray of sunshine, depending on one's perspective. After completing three years of Ted Kennedy's term, Brown lost his bid for a full term to Elizabeth Warren, who won 53 percent of the vote to Brown's 46 percent.

After Brown's defeat, many were surprised when he opted not to run in the 2013 special election to fill John Kerry's Senate seat after Kerry resigned to become US secretary of state, and again decided not to run for Bay State governor in 2014. Instead, he turned north. Like many families in the Seacoast, Merrimack Valley, and North Shore regions of New Hampshire and Massachusetts, Brown's family ties span the two states. Having moved to Massachusetts as a little boy, Brown returned to New Hampshire often to visit his grandparents, where his mother and sister still live. He and his wife purchased a 1,700-square-foot vacation home in Rye in 1993. He became a registered New Hampshire voter at the end of 2013. By early 2014 Scott Brown was priming to run in the senatorial campaign in his new state against incumbent Democrat Jeanne Shaheen. But in doing so, he invited a media firestorm over his status as carpetbagger.

## MEDIA FRAMING AND THE CARPETBAGGER TROPE

The media play an important role in the process of disseminating information and shaping the images they convey. Those involved in "making, reporting, and editing news have an incentive to shape it so as to attract audiences and, sometimes, to encourage particular interpretations through its content and form" (Edelman 1988, 90). Tactically, the media's construction of reality through the creation of meanings is a "critical element in political maneuver" that allows the legitimating of action and the construction of "beliefs about the significance of events, of problems, of crises, of policy changes, and of leaders" (Edelman 1985). The media thus give events meaning. Therefore, the media play a decisive role in our understanding of everyday life and our interpretation of such life through the creation of meaning and application to events.

The media distribute information through framing tactics (Tuchman 1978; Gamson and Lasch 1983; Gamson and Modigliani 1989; Neuman, Just, and Crigler 1992; Parenti 1993; Schudson 2003; Bennett 2003) and agenda setting—the act of helping the reader/audience decide what is important to think about—thus affecting decision making by the public and policymakers (Cook et al. 1983; Bennett 2003). Any story consists of two parts: (1) frames, and (2) a justification for position (Gamson and Lasch 1983, 398). Frames or packages are "conceptual tools which media rely on to convey, interpret and evaluate information" and therefore are a central concept to studying the media (Tuchman 1978; Gamson and Modigliani 1989; Neuman, Just, and Crigler 1992; Parenti 1993; Schudson 2003; Bennett 2003).

All frames-packages have an internal structure that organizes the frame for making sense of the event, and then use symbols to relay the meaning (Gamson and Modigliani 1989). Frames are an organizational tool that allows the comprehension of problems at hand (Gamson and Lasch 1983) and are used to choose, accentuate, and connect elements in a story that are consistent with a proposed broader perspective. For example, Gamson and Lasch use images and language elements such as metaphors to encompass their framework on social welfare policy, whereas Neuman et al. employ conceptual frames like economics, conflict, and morality to study political discourse (Gamson and Lasch 1983; Neuman, Just, and Crigler 1992). According to Gitlin (1980, 7) "media frames...organize the world both for journalists who report it and, in some important degree, for us who rely on their reports."

In the 2014 midterm New Hampshire senatorial race, the media employed carpetbagger rhetoric and construction to highlight Scott Brown's attempt to be the next New Hampshire senator. To assess the extent of the carpetbagger framing of Brown's campaign, we analyzed content in news articles, radio broadcasts, and campaign messages in the Granite State starting in March of 2014 up to the November election. The analysis drew attention to themes and issues connected with Brown's carpetbagger status. For Berelson (1952), "the theme is among the most useful units of content analysis, particularly for the study of the effect of communications upon public opinion, because it takes the form in which issues and attitudes are usually discussed" (139). Themes, thus, help frame an article. We discovered several themes in the carpetbagger discussion of Scott Brown: (1) rhetorical attachment of the term *carpetbagger* is not universal, (2) territory and affiliation matter in carpetbagger rhetoric, and (3) carpetbaggers as political con artists.

## NOT A UNIVERSAL CONSTRUCTION: CARPETBAGGERS AND POLITICAL CANDIDATES

What makes a candidate a true resident and able to represent citizens emerged quickly in the media discourse. Both Jeanne Shaheen and Scott Brown were not native born to the Granite State. But Brown's recent employment as the senator from Massachusetts allowed media outlets to instantaneously say that, "Hey, this guy's not from New Hampshire"

(Peoples 2014). In another story (Peoples 2014), readers could find the following observations: "'New Hampshire people want New Hampshire people,' said a 52-year-old patron at Manchester's famed Red Arrow Diner as Brown pressed the flesh nearby, 'He's not really a New Hampshire person. He's a politician from Massachusetts.'" Brown came inside the diner, the story reports, swung his legs over a stool at the counter and sat next to the patron. Even though she promised not to vote for incumbent Democrat US Senator Jeanne Shaheen, a former two-term governor, "she pointedly questioned Brown's devotion to New Hampshire. Behind him, 71-year-old Connie Antoniou whispered, 'I wish the Massachusetts people would stay in Massachusetts.'" Brown reminded the patron—and maybe Antoniou, who was within earshot—that "carpetbagger is a derogatory term in New Hampshire given that roughly 60 percent of its people were born elsewhere, including the current and former Democratic governors. Governor Maggie Hassan arrived in 1989, from Massachusetts, born in Boston, while Shaheen, born in Missouri, has lived here for more than 40 years" (Peoples 2014).

Brown made a legitimate point about residency, but he omitted the important fact that neither Hassan nor Sheehan made such an obvious and immediate move for political purposes. They entered Granite State politics gradually, thus taking the edge off the outsider, flatlander, and carpetbagger perception. As the *Concord Monitor* observed, "New Hampshire and Massachusetts have a complicated relationship. They share a state line, professional sports teams and a major media market, but there are traces of resentment among some New Hampshire natives. Thousands of Massachusetts residents moved into New Hampshire in recent years, drawn by lower taxes and cheaper real estate. The migration helped give Democrats a slight voter registration edge [as of this writing], although the state is considered far more balanced politically than solidly Democratic Massachusetts" (Fitzgerald 2011). Transplanted Bay State residents likely would join current commonwealth residents in observing that New Hampshire has marketed its "NH Advantage" lifestyle, tourism, and vacation opportunities aggressively and has profited from the local taxes new residents pay. Moreover, they might observe that New Hampshire is economically dependent on Massachusetts with more than 100,000 Granite Staters working south of the border. Throw in Logan International

Airport, the Greater Boston medical, educational, and technology complex and Cape Cod, and Massachusetts might just as reasonably claim that it gets its fill of New Hampshire every day (Fitzgerald 2011).

In a speech before the Nashua Rotary Club, Brown reminded listeners that his family roots go back "nine generations" in New Hampshire. Only the night before, he had seen Republican and Democratic protesters lift up a bright yellow sign reading "Brownbagger, go home to Mass" (Haddadin 2013). PolitiFact New Hampshire, a fact-checking agency, observed that on Brown's mother's side, the Ruggs had lived in the Granite State for several generations and one branch of the family may have resided here as early as 1634. It may not help that a key family name is Rugg, a name which, without its final "g," becomes a a synonym for "carpet." In any event, PolitiFact NH rated Brown's claim as "half-true" (Haddadin 2013).

## POLITICAL REGIONS VERSUS STATES: TERRITORY AND AFFILIATION MATTER

The carpetbagger issue underlines the question of territoriality and affiliation in American politics. Contemporary issues of media markets, polling zones, market saturation, social media, and globalization have their place, but old-fashioned concerns over "Where are you from?," "Why are you here?," and "What have you done?" have not disappeared. For New Hampshire and states like it, the perception of a stable community where many residents have long, even historic roots, is widespread. Membership in such a community means paying taxes, holding a job, volunteering, participating in town meetings, and standing for election. Taking the kids to soccer practice, cheering the football team, helping at the church food pantry, knowing neighbors, and ringing the bell for the Salvation Army are just as important as positions on immigration reform, border security, Iraq and Afghanistan, and job stimulation. Electorally, retail politics matters and thrives in New Hampshire. Voters expect to meet those seeking the US presidency, and they want to know, really know those who actually represent *them* in Congress. Ironically, as New Hampshire becomes more, not less, like her big neighbor to the immediate south, the perception and the ideology of the "New Hampshire way," the "New Hampshire difference," become increasingly important. We are we because we are not you and you are, most assuredly, not us—at least to us. Got it? The carpetbagger trope is one significant defense of the imaginary turf and way of life.

As the campaign developed, the carpetbagger/residency issue did not go away. John DiStaso's column "Granite Status," published by the *Manchester Union Leader*'s *New Hampshire Sunday News*, picked up the *Concord Monitor* story posted by the Associated Press. Brown told the AP, "Do I have the best credentials? Probably not. 'Cause, you know, whatever. But I have long and strong ties to this state. People know." DiStaso added, "The nonchalant comment went viral on social media, made the talk show circuit and was even brought up none other than late-night television talk host Jimmy Fallon. Fallon suggested a few Brown slogans of his own, including, 'Scott Brown for Senate. Or whoever. Whatever. Forever." Shaheen, MSNBC, Joe Scarborough, Hotair.com, and others all had some fun with it. Brown's comments did not do much to eliminate the perception that he was a "suit," a "jock," and, of course, a "carpetbagger." DiStaso also points out that Brown, who voted against ending big oil and gas subsidies while in the Senate in 2012 and who later received nearly $35,000 from oil and natural gas PACs, had not yet signed the "People's Pledge" to keep corporate oil money out of the New Hampshire Senate race in 2014 (DiStaso 2014).

In early June, the *Concord Monitor* wrote an editorial calling on Brown to open up about his relationship to a firm called Global Digital Solutions Inc., which a year earlier had named the former senator to its board and given him stock worth $1.3 million at the time. The *Monitor*, quoting a *Boston Globe* report, claimed that "descriptions of the company's business practices serve as a garden of red flags for would-be investors." The editorial continued, "As a private citizen, Brown is entitled to seek his fortune, but as a seeker of public office he owes the people a proper accounting. To wait a month before voters must choose the Republican who will challenge Sen. Jeanne Shaheen is the worst kind of political sleight of hand." To add to the pressure, however, the editorial began by observing, "Scott Brown may have finally found a way to get the 'carpetbagger' chorus to change its tune, but he probably won't like the new song much better. In fact, he may develop a sentimental fondness for the good old days when people merely questioned his geographical commitment to the Granite State" (*Concord Monitor* 2014).

## NOT FOOLING THE (MAJORITY OF) VOTERS: CARPETBAGGERS AS CON ARTISTS

Another key site for discussion of the carpetbagger claim was the letters section of New Hampshire newspapers and websites. Sometimes, even when residency itself was not the key issue—and, indeed, the issue slipped from top billing as the campaign moved forward—Brown's tenure in New Hampshire still found its way into the discussion. Jim Mayotte, writing on behalf of Brown from Sanbornton, rapped Shaheen over the VA scandal, Obamacare, and the Benghazi consulate attack. Mayotte, who declares that he is a veteran and a life member of the National Rifle Association (NRA), observes, "I have read that Scott Brown is a 'carpetbagger.' His last name is not Clinton or Kennedy" (Mayotte 2014). Rhetorically, Mayotte makes his pro-Brown points, but his reference functions like a boomerang, renewing the residency issue, but failing to dispatch it. Shaheen may have her problems, but she is not in the same moving van as Hillary Clinton or Robert F. Kennedy, both of whom relocated to New York and declared residency so they could run and win US Senate seats from the Empire State in 2000 and 1964 respectively. Brown, meanwhile, did precisely what Clinton and Kennedy did.

In another opinion piece, Pamela Faltin of Durham is hostile to Brown in her letter. She writes that she wonders "how gullible Scott Brown thinks the electorate of New Hampshire is" (Faltin 2014). She cites his sudden discovery of "our lovely state" and new residency, along with failure to take the pledge against outside money even when he once supported it in Massachusetts. "Brown has already proven that he doesn't know much about New Hampshire voters. He doesn't realize that we take elections seriously here. We think for ourselves. We make our own decisions. We cannot be brainwashed by attack ads funded by wealthy special interest groups, but we can spot a carpetbagger from miles away" (Faltin 2014). "Most people move to New Hampshire for the quality of life, the mountains, lakes, forests, oceans, no sales or income tax and good jobs," writes Tom Kamberis of Hillsborough. "Brown 'moved' here for one thing and one thing only: to run for office. Republicans are so desperate to win an election, they are willing to sell out the people of New Hampshire to a carpetbagger" (Kamberis 2014).

By the time of the Republican primary on September 9, even though the carpetbagger issue was well established in the campaign rhetoric, Brown swept to a convincing win. According to Manchester's WMUR-TV, he won 50 percent of the vote with nearly 60,000 votes, easily outdistancing Jim Rubens and former US Senator Bob Smith, each with 23 percent. In some respects, however, intra-Republican carpetbagger complaints made the Democrats the real winner.

Even though other issues rose to the surface, Brown's remarks and gaffes kept the political geography and carpetbagger issue alive. On a Boston Herald Radio show, Brown observed, "And that's a big difference between Sen. Shaheen and me and many other people in the Massachusetts delegation, and Sen. Shaheen, in particular, the president." But Brown, of course, was running in New Hampshire, not Massachusetts (Itkowitz 2014).

The Brown campaign attacked Shaheen for not standing with President Obama, with whom she voted 100 percent of the time in Brown's telling of it, when the president was "in town." The only problem was that, properly speaking, New Hampshire is Shaheen's backyard, not Massachusetts—and Obama was speaking in Worcester, fifty miles from the New Hampshire border. "When asked about this gaffe, the Brown campaign responded with one of the worst excuses ever. They claimed that by 'in town,' they meant in New England, even though New England is a region, not a town. The truth is that the Brown people don't know [in] what state they are running. Scott Brown lives in Massachusetts. He was a senator from Massachusetts. It makes sense that his campaign would still be thinking Massachusetts" (Easley 2014).

During an October 29 debate on WMUR-TV, Manchester, Brown was asked about economic issues in Sullivan County, located in western New Hampshire. Brown's answers suggested that he thought Sullivan was in the North Country. The moderator clarified, and Brown said he was talking "about any place past Concord, actually, and the challenges of our state." The moderator interjected again that Sullivan is west of Concord. In fact, Sullivan is both north and west of the capital city. The moderator acknowledged his error later that night and apologized—but Brown was left looking confused (Ballhaus 2014).

Sometimes Brown's mistakes in local knowledge were not even his fault. In late October, *Foster's Daily Democrat* in Dover published a rebuke of Shaheen over high gasoline prices, claiming that Shaheen was part of the problem. The rebuke, rebutting recent points the incumbent senator had made in an exchange with Brown, came from former, and now deceased, House Speaker Marshall Cobleigh. The problem for Brown was that the op-ed piece, originally published in 2008 in the *Union Leader*, came from the state Republican Party headquarters, which had noted its date and the status of the author. But when it was published, Cobleigh's 2009 death had been omitted. Joan McCarter, writing in the *Daily Kos*, asks, "Could it be that they can't find any high profile Republicans who are also from New Hampshire who are willing to write op-eds in support of Scott Brown, the guy from Massachusetts" (McCarter 2014).

## CARPETBAGGER RHETORIC IN ADVERTISEMENTS

Writing op-ed pieces, editorials, and letters, of course, is only one part of a complete rhetorical campaign strategy. The dynamic audiovisual component, as seen in television advertisements, in short films, on social media, and in YouTube repostings is another central element. Throughout many of the Brown and Shaheen videos, an effort either to refute the carpetbagger image or to employ it is clearly visible. New Hampshire may be depicted subtly or overtly, but it is on the screen of the home computer, the iPhone, and the tablet for each and every viewer to see, forward, review, and repost. Here are four videos to consider, two for each candidate.

In his "New Day" film, Brown attacks Shaheen for supporting Obama, denounces problems with cancellation of healthcare plans, and berates joblessness and the scandal in veterans' healthcare. One sequence, semiotically saturated with New Hampshire icons—barns, mountains, foliage, lakes, Dartmouth, veterans, and construction workers—envelops the viewer with a sense that here is a candidate for the average worker, a candidate who knows where he is from and understands why he is going to DC. The voice-over has Brown declaring, "I will answer only to the people of New Hampshire and will not forget who sent me there. I will strive each and every day to make New Hampshire proud" (YouTube 2014b).

Another pro-Brown video, relying heavily on fall foliage, tackles the residency issue head-on: born at Portsmouth Naval Shipyard (ignoring its Kittery, Maine, location), mother a waitress at Hampton Beach and father an airman at Pease Air Force Base, homeowner and taxpayer in Rye for twenty years, wants to confront the healthcare plan that Obama and Shaheen "forced on us" with "few options," and wants to "preserve New Hampshire's way of life" by helping employers add jobs and helping Washington understand "when to get out of the way" (YouTube 2014a).

Brown's ads make effective points, but they faced Shaheen's, which underline her deep New Hampshire experience. In one thirty-minute spot, titled "New Hampshire First," she has a series of short vignettes, talking heads that are iconically Granite State: A Portsmouth Naval Shipyard worker, the mayor of Berlin, a woman from Barrington, a citizen at the Portsmouth Memorial Bridge, and a young woman at the Manchester Job Corps Center—all associated with projects that Shaheen has helped support. A speaker from Milan reminds viewers that "she fights for the people of New Hampshire" (YouTube 2014c). In a powerful and surprising minute-long piece, Ursula Gordon from New Boston tells viewers that, although she is a registered Republican, she supports Shaheen who helped get the local bank off her back after her husband became seriously ill and they had trouble making mortgage payments. "I wouldn't be in this house if it weren't for Jeanne Shaheen. She's the one who got the job done. She's the one who cared." The ad deftly reminds viewers of the value of longevity in a place, the power of history and connections—all things that Scott Brown might have in Massachusetts but not in New Hampshire (YouTube 2014d).

As Election Day drew near, a *Concord Monitor* (2014c) story observed that "Brown's favorability numbers are just as dismal [as Shaheen's]—one poll shows voters liking him less the more they get to know him—he's running neck-and-neck with the considerably more popular Shaheen. 'It's really not a matter of either candidate's popularity. It's a matter of President Obama's popularity,' said Andrew Smith, director of the University of New Hampshire Survey Center. People don't pay much attention to the particulars of mid-term election politics,' he added. 'Their sense of politics is what's going on with the president,' he said. 'They like what the president's doing or they don't like what the president's doing.'"

By Election Day, more than $36 million had been spent on the race, including $24 million by outside groups, many of them fueled by Republican efforts to regain control of the US Senate, something that proved to be successful no thanks to New Hampshire. According to the nonpartisan Center for Public Integrity, $10 million alone had been spent on New

Hampshire advertising, split roughly evenly between the GOP and the Democrats for some 15,000 ads (*Concord Monitor* 2014b).

When the results were in, it was clear that Shaheen had survived Brown's assault. Amid more substantive issues, the residency question persisted, acting as a kind of hot seasoning that put voters off. The *Concord Monitor* opined, "Brown, for all his charm and 'regular guy' appeal, never truly shed the carpetbagger label that adorned his candidacy from day one. Even moderates and Independents who wanted to embrace anybody but Shaheen couldn't shake the feeling that the state wasn't as close to Brown's heart as he claimed it was and as it should be. That made his attempts to paint Shaheen as somebody out of touch with New Hampshire voters appear all the more comical" (*Concord Monitor* 2014b). Discussing the wave of Republican victories in November, the *Monitor* cautioned, "State Democrats are no doubt rejoicing that the national wave was more like a ripple here, but they would be wise not to misread the results. There is no blue wall [around New Hampshire], just a purple haze" (*Concord Monitor* 2014b). The residency pot was stirred again when Brown's campaign was accused of using a mere green background with stock footage for some of his campaign ads, instead of real New Hampshire landscapes (*Concord Monitor* 2014b).

Meanwhile, Dan Tuohy of Manchester's *Union Leader* observed, "Brown did everything in his power to fashion the mid-term election as a referendum on President Barack Obama, who continues to have low approval ratings in the state.... Shortly after establishing his residency, Brown began establishing his Live Free or Die bona fides. But the transition was not entirely seamless, beginning with remarks he made last December when he called New Hampshire the 'Live Free AND Die' state. With or without New Hampshire license plates on his GMC pickup truck, Democrats zeroed in on the carpetbagger label. [Introducing Hillary Clinton at a campaign event in Nashua], Shaheen quipped, 'She traveled 956,000 miles as Secretary of State. That's nearly as many miles as Scott Brown traveled looking for a Senate seat to buy'" (Tuohy 2014).

Perhaps the most ungracious, though pertinent, carpetbagger-related question came in the waning hours of the race, when MSNBC host Alex Wagner asked Brown if he was planning to return to Massachusetts if he lost. Brown remained silent (Freelander 2014).

## CONCLUSION

Residency, in its carpetbagger's guise, is not an issue that most politicians must confront. Scott Brown's self-confidence in the face of Obama's eroding national support, his own 2010 Senate success, and his audacious hope, to steal a phrase from President Obama, led him north to try again for membership in the world's most exclusive club. The members of the club do not determine their membership, the people of each state do—and that meant Brown had to employ all the political and rhetorical muscle he could use to change voter perceptions in a state that often delights in tweaking its large, urban neighbor to the south. Brown succeeded in the Republican primary, but ironically some of the very concerns raised by fellow party members were picked up and made politically toxic for him in the general election.

Ordinary voters, state and national media reporters in print, television, radio, and online, late night talk show hosts, and Democratic and Republican political operatives would not let the issue rest. Every Brown gaffe and misstep, and there are dozens of them in any campaign, resurrected the Granite State/Bay State question.

In many ways, Brown's failure is an object lesson in the challenges that carpetbagger candidates face, wherever they run. To succeed in a new state when one is a newly arrived candidate and former officeholder elsewhere, a carpetbagger, it is particularly helpful, if not determinative, that the candidate be (1) widely perceived as competent for the job; (2) possessed of bona fide connections to the new jurisdiction; (3) free of baggage and impediments, including service in a previous electoral district perceived with some hostility by the new voters; (4) entrusted with the support of his or her party establishment; (5) free of a contest against a popular, entrenched "local" candidate; and (6) conscious of shifting moods and factors in and beyond the electoral district in question.

The first thing New Hampshire voters learned about Brown in his 2014 campaign was the fact that he was a recent transplant from Massachusetts, and had only moved to New Hampshire because of his 2012 loss in Massachusetts. Brown's efforts to focus on his family and childhood ties to the state only served to draw attention to his status as a carpetbagger, and his Republican and Democratic opponents alike were only too happy to continue to remind voters of that status throughout the campaign. Normally, campaign ads full of local color draw little notice; for a carpetbagger, these ads remind voters that the candidate is not from around here. And every reminder makes it hard for the carpetbagger to focus on anything other than his or her problematic status.

This is doubly so for the carpetbagger who is not only a newcomer to a state but, like Brown, has actually held office in another state. Jeanne Shaheen may have been born in Missouri, but she was not the senator from Missouri before she ran for office in New Hampshire. In addition to making the fact of one's carpetbagger status more vivid in the minds of voters, holding office saddles the carpetbagger with all the drawbacks of holding office (such as a record with controversial or difficult votes) and none of the benefits (such as a history of constituent service or a relationship with voters developed over many election cycles).

Did Scott Brown's carpetbagger status cost him the election? In one sense, this question is impossible to answer. We cannot rerun the election to make Brown a lifelong New Hampshirite and see what happens. But we can look at seven other Senate races throughout the country in which a first-term Democrat sought reelection. In three of these races—those in Alaska, Colorado, and North Carolina—the Democratic incumbent lost. In the races in Minnesota, New Mexico, Oregon, and Virginia, the incumbent survived (very narrowly, in Virginia's case). As a state where presidential elections are often closely contested and both parties are competitive at all levels of office, New Hampshire is a better fit with the first group of states than the latter. Shaheen's victory in a year when Democrats generally fared poorly outside of reliably Democratic states provides reason to believe that Brown's carpetbagger status was a meaningful drag on his candidacy. This election thus demonstrates the importance of place in American politics, and suggests that while many aspects of midterm elections have been nationalized, voters continue to be deeply skeptical of those who cross state lines to run for office.

# Voting Process

Chapter 7

# Assessing Recommendations of the Presidential Commission on Election Administration on Reducing Long Lines and Wait Times on Election Day

*Terri Susan Fine and Charles Stewart III*

In his 2012 Election Night acceptance speech, President Barack Obama expressed concern about long lines at the polls. "I want to thank every American who participated in this election whether you voted for the first time, or waited in line for a very long time. By the way, we have to fix that."[1]

President Obama reinforced his concern in his State of the Union message the following February.

> Defending our freedom, though, is not just the job of our military alone. We must all do our part to make sure our God-given rights are protected here at home. That includes one of the most fundamental rights of a democracy: the right to vote. When any American, no matter where they live or what their party, are denied that right because they can't afford to wait for five or six or seven hours just to cast their ballot, we are betraying our ideals.[2]

The next month, President Obama signed Executive Order 13639 establishing the Presidential Commission on Election Administration (PCEA) "in order to promote the efficient administration of Federal elections." E.O. 13639 identified eleven areas of concern including "the number, location, management, operation and design of polling places."[3]

This chapter considers the PCEA's concern about long lines through three lenses. First, what are the legislative and human factors impacting line length, and how does line length vary across states and demographic groups? Second, how is public opinion and political participation impacted by line length? Finally, what are the opportunities and limitations associated with President Obama's desire to address long lines?

To answer this last question, we focus on a large, ethnically and racially diverse Florida county within the context of national and state factors. Florida has been subjected to intense scrutiny especially since the 2000 General Election. The issues exposed there were not new to Florida or other states. It was the consequence of these issues that invited scrutiny. Among other concerns plaguing Florida that year and the three presidential elections since, have been long lines at polling places (US Commission on Civil Rights 2001). Even though federal and state election laws enacted since 2000 have targeted concerns in Florida and elsewhere, including voter experiences, Florida had the worst national wait-time record in 2012.

## NATIONAL CONTOURS OF LONG LINES

A thorough PCEA report released in January 2014 outlined best practices for election administrators, giving specific attention to voter experiences including poll wait times. The commission called for greater attention to polling-place congestion because long wait times suggest a fundamental mismatch between the number of voters and the resources allocated to accommodate them.

> The image of voters waiting for six or more hours to vote on Election Day 2012, as in the two previous Presidential contests, spurred the call for reform that led to creation of this Commission. Research suggests that, although a limited number of jurisdictions experienced long wait times, over five million voters in 2012 experienced wait times exceeding one hour and an additional five million waited between a half hour and

an hour. In some jurisdictions, the problem has recurred for several presidential elections, while in others, a particular confluence of factors led to unprecedented lines in 2012. It became clear to the Commission as it investigated this problem that there is no single cause for long lines and there is no single solution. But the problem is solvable. (Presidential Commission on Election Administration 2014, 13)

Several related factors contribute to longer wait times including ballot length, which is impacted by federal, state, and local laws. The longer it takes individuals to vote the longer will be the time that others wait in line.

Two federal laws impacting ballot length include the 1872 law setting a uniform presidential and congressional election date to take place on the first Tuesday after the first Monday in November in even-numbered years. Presidential election ballots now almost always include a US House of Representatives race (Maskell 2004, 4),[4] while some but not all states will include a US Senate race in presidential election years due to staggered Senate terms.[5] The 1965 Voting Rights Act as amended in 1975 increases ballot length by requiring those counties with at least 5 percent of persons speaking a language other than English at home (based on US Census data) to provide bilingual ballots.[6] In most jurisdictions, this is implemented by printing multiple languages on a common ballot—voters do not choose from among ballots each with an eligible language. Election officials in counties nearing the 5 percent minimum anticipate need by providing ballots in that language.[7] Ballot-casting options also impact wait times. Pre–Election Day voting options include absentee voting, early in-person voting ("EIPV"/"early voting"), or vote by mail. Two-thirds of all states, plus the District of Columbia, enjoy the EIPV option while every state offers absentee balloting (National Council of State Legislatures 2015). The fewer hours that polls are open limit voters' Election Day options, which may impact wait times. Polls in forty-two states are open at least twelve hours while polls are open fewer than ten hours in four states (Ostermeier 2014). State and local ballots may include constitutional amendments or referenda, which will lengthen ballots and potentially increase ballot completion time. Wait times will naturally be affected.

Human factors relating to voters and poll workers impact wait times. Voters studying their ballot in advance will need less ballot completion time compared with those seeing their ballot for the first time on Election Day. Sample ballots may be available online, in local newspapers, or mailed by local elections offices. Voters who are unfamiliar with various ballot design aspects and voting machines may also slow down the voting process.

Human factors also impact how poll workers handle election equipment. States and localities continue experimenting with election equipment to improve the efficiency and accuracy of checking in and casting ballots (see Claassen et al. 2008). Poll-worker skills must accommodate these changes to minimize procedural errors. Still, poll-worker availability is impacted by federal Election Day scheduling requirements that limit opportunities for younger, tech-savvy populations, such as college students, to be available for twelve or more hours on a Tuesday that falls in the middle of a typical college semester (Bryer et al. 2011; Fine and Jewett 2008). State level voter identification requirements also impact wait times. Poll workers must verify appropriate identification types, and that the identification provided belongs to the person producing it (such as matching signatures or photographs).[8]

Long lines vary across states and demographic cohorts. According to the 2012 Survey of the Performance of American Elections, wait times were the longest in Florida, Virginia, South Carolina, and Maryland while the shortest lines were in Vermont, Alaska, and South Dakota (see fig. 7.1) that year (Stewart 2013a). The national average was 14 minutes. Comparing the four largest population states, California (6 minutes), New York (10 minutes), and Texas (12 minutes) had wait times lower than the 14-minute national average while wait times in Florida, at 45 minutes, exceeded all other states (US General Accounting Office Report 2014).

Voters in urban areas, at 18 minutes, wait longer than voters in either rural, at 8 minutes, or suburban areas, at 12 minutes, while minority voters tend to wait almost twice as long as whites. Wait times across racial groups also varied as whites waited 13 minutes on average while African Americans and Hispanics averaged over 20 minutes wait time (Peters 2013, A1).

Long wait times in general and varying wait times across political, demographic, and racial groups, warrant consideration as voters are not equally impacted. In 2012, 500,000 to 700,000 potential voters may not have voted because of long lines and polling-place problems (Stewart 2013b). Voters waiting the longest express the least confidence that their

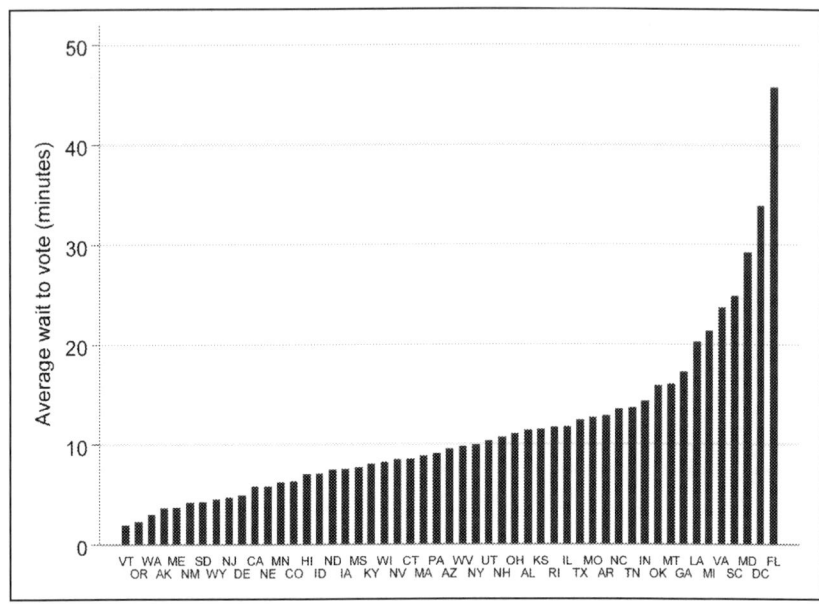

**Figure 7.1.** 2012 Survey of the Performance of American Elections

*Source: 2012 Survey of the Performance of American Elections*[9]

vote will count. Voters not waiting a long time, but living in states with long lines, report lower confidence in the vote count (Gronke 2014; Stewart and Ansolabehere 2015).

### LONG LINES IN FLORIDA

At the most fundamental level, long lines result from insufficient capacity of polling-place resources—voting machines, poll books, election workers, and other factors—to handle the influx of voters. Queuing theory is the science of studying whether systems can handle customer influx, which has been applied to many commercial settings, but rarely to electoral environments.[10] Here, we report results of observational research conducted in one Florida county in 2014 that was aimed at applying queuing principles to diagnosing line problems in that state.

Problems experienced elsewhere were especially pronounced in Florida in 2012. According to the *Orlando Sentinel,* "The long Election Day lines around Florida may have turned away more than 200,000 frustrated would-be voters who gave up ... before they cast ballots—or else saw the lines and elected not to join them." Nearly two million registered Florida voters live in precincts that stayed open at least ninety minutes past the scheduled 7 P.M. closing time, including over 500,000 voters whose precincts remained open at least three hours past the 7 P.M. closing time (Powers and Damron 2013).

The county we studied was given the fictitious name of Magnolia County.[11] Magnolia County is home to approximately one million of Florida's 19.8 million residents and covers over eight hundred square miles. Between 2000 and 2014, the Magnolia County population grew 3 percent faster than the rest of the state. As of 2010, slightly less than half of the county's residents are white, with African Americans constituting about 21 percent and Hispanics making up roughly one-quarter of the county population. One-third of the residents speak a language other than English at home;[12] 11 percent live below the poverty line.[13]

Although Magnolia County has more registered Democrats (41 percent) than Republicans (28 percent) or "No Party Affiliation" (25 percent), election returns typically situate Magnolia County as a swing county in a swing state. Its congressional delegation is split between Republicans and Democrats, while its state legislators include some of the most influential state Republican leaders.

Florida's long lines were particularly problematic in Magnolia County. Along with an adjacent county, Magnolia was one of Florida's counties with the longest lines in 2012, with almost half of those voting living in precincts that closed at least ninety minutes late (Powers and Damron 2013).

Magnolia County 2012 wait times suggest that it would be an ideal laboratory to evaluate some concerns expressed by the president and the PCEA. Analyzing voter experiences in Magnolia County might also shed light on the opportunities and limitations associated with wait-time reduction proposals.

Magnolia County wait times were studied on Election Day 2014 as part of the Polling Process of the Future Project (PPOTF), which also conducted similar studies in four other locations around the country.[14] The purpose of the study was to gather data to assist local elections officials in their effort to reduce wait times. The Magnolia County study involved five teams of students visiting twenty randomly selected election precincts across five county commission districts. Students spent between two and three hours at each of their four assigned precincts.[15] Students observed line length at result intervals in the polling process and observed individual voters moving through the process.

Specific attention was paid to how long it took voters to reach the check-in table and to check in, how long it took voters to complete their ballot, and how long it took voters to cast their ballot once completed. Each point in the voting process represents different factors contributing to overall voting time. The check-in stage speaks to factors associated with poll-worker responsibility for determining voter eligibility and establishing proper identification,[16] locating voters in the statewide voter database as needed, and monitoring voters as they sign in. Voters may secure voting assistance at check-in or may be asked to provide a signature if they registered online or if the signature differs significantly from the signature produced with their identification. It is at check-in that voters are issued a ballot about which they may have questions.

Compliance with Voting Rights Act amendments has led Magnolia County to print bilingual ballots in both Spanish and English, which makes the ballot twice as long as it might otherwise be, and more difficult to navigate. Florida also uses the office-block ballot design, which slows down voters who wish to cast a straight-ticket ballot. Florida runs consolidated elections in even-numbered years, which places federal, state, and local offices together on a ballot with state constitutional amendments and charter revisions listed last. Florida election law requires that candidates whose party is the same as the governor's be listed first for each office followed by candidates representing the other major party. Only Republicans have served as Florida governor since 1999 so all federal and state Republican candidates are listed before all Democratic candidates, followed by Independent and minor-party candidates. Candidate names may be listed out of alphabetical order, which may confuse some voters who are searching for specific names.

State constitutional amendment rules also contribute to ballot length and confusion. There are five ways to add amendments to the ballot in Florida. Amendments proposed through citizen petition are limited to seventy-five words while amendments added by the state legislature are not subject to word limits. Amendments proposed by the state legislature often exceed five hundred words. Ballot length, as it pertains to bilingual requirements and the number and source of constitutional amendments, and the office-block ballot design, can each add to the time it takes to complete ballots.

The last part of the voting process includes waiting to place the ballot into the tabulator machine, which requires inserting it into a horizontal slot and may confuse some voters. (Magnolia County tabulators allow ballots to be inserted right side up or upside down, or from either direction.)

Data on each stage in the voting process was collected separately during the entire 7:00 A.M.–7:00 P.M. state-mandated voting period.[17] The study results provide a snapshot of wait times and illuminate some factors impacting wait times across Magnolia County. In 2014, voters arrived at an average of 1.1 per minute, with the average number of people waiting in line during any given five-minute period of 4.8. (The typical precinct had three poll books for checking in voters although about 10 percent of precincts were given a fourth poll book due to precinct size.)[18] These voters took an average of 2 minutes and 8 seconds to check in. After checking in, voters took an average of 8 minutes and 5 seconds to vote and 1 minute and 2 seconds to scan their ballots. All told, voters spent an average of 11 minutes and 22 seconds in the polling place, from check-in to departure.[19]

Statistics derived by this research may be used to calculate an estimate of the average wait time prior to check-in using "Little's Law," a cornerstone of queuing theory.[20] Little's Law suggests a 7.1 minute average wait time, which is very close to the 7.3 minute statewide average reported by Florida respondents to the 2014 Survey of the Performance of American Elections (Stewart 2015).[21]

We can use other tools grounded in queuing theory to illustrate the challenges Magnolia County would face in presidential elections including the "Line Optimization and Poll Worker Management" application developed by Stephen Graves and published on the PCEA website.[22] This tool uses the "M/M/c" model to estimate average wait times given three inputs: arrival rates, check-in times, and number of check-in stations. In Magnolia County these inputs would be an arrival rate of sixty-six voters per hour with two minutes to check in at three check-in stations. The "Graves Tool" estimates an average 81-second wait before check-in.

In presidential election years, Magnolia County turnout is about 50 percent greater than in midterms. Thus, if the arrival rate were 50 percent greater, at ninety-nine voters per hour, with the same two-minute check-in time at three check-in stations, the average wait time is infinity (*sic*). That is, the simulation indicates that the line will grow throughout the day, never reach a steady state, and only dissipate after the polls have closed.

The results suggest that Magnolia County's capacity, on average, is sufficient during midterm elections to check in voters well within the PCEA suggested benchmark of a thirty-minute maximum. The same models also suggest that check-in capacity is insufficient to handle presidential Election Day rush within the same benchmark. To achieve that, the average Magnolia County Election Day polling place would need an additional poll book.

Financial considerations would challenge implementation. Adding poll books not only adds costs but also adds to the space needed for any polling place, making some current polling places too small. Alternately, maintaining current polling places justifies adding polling places, which creates greater recruitment and financial issues for election supervisors to hire and pay more poll workers.

Reducing ballot completion time is problematic for political reasons. It is likely that state legislators will not forfeit their option to produce lengthy constitutional amendments nor is it likely that the Republican-dominated state legislature will alphabetize candidate names at the expense of listing Republican candidates first for federal and state offices.[23]

Ballot scanning takes the least amount of time although reducing that time would likely raise voter concerns about election integrity. Magnolia County tabulators rarely jam although telephonic technical support and roving field service technicians are available throughout the day. Speeding up this phase of the process would require using the "Emergency Ballot Box," a metal box in which voters place ballots that are later scanned. Concerns about integrity would increase as voters wonder whether their ballot would be cast or counted if it was placed in the Emergency Ballot Box.

## CONCLUSION: LOOKING TO FUTURE MIDTERM AND PRESIDENTIAL ELECTIONS

Midterm polling experiences differ from presidential polling experiences. Long lines and associated wait times in 2012 were not evident in 2014. Several factors contributed to shorter wait times in 2014 mimicking the 2012 fourteen-minute national average, including lower turnout and more experienced voters who typically vote in midterm elections compared with presidential election voters who tend to be both less experienced and less active voters. Midterm elections bring low public and media attention while presidential elections tend to attract high public and media attention. Further, the absence of a presidential or US Senate race in 2014 in Florida depressed voter turnout because voters were less likely to know who was running or for what office. Nonetheless, by observing the voting process in 2014, we have established that the insights of queuing theory are relevant for understanding the dynamics of long lines, thus we are in a position to understand how future midterm and presidential elections might unfold.

Presidential election years increase turnout for all offices on the ballot because the high-stimulus nature of the presidential race draws voters to the polls (Panagopoulos 2011). High-stimulus elections also draw less-experienced and less-informed voters to the polls. Low turnout voters may be less comfortable voting, confused with various aspects of ballot design, unfamiliar with the substance of proposed constitutional amendments, and take longer to complete their ballot. Such voters may more likely be unaware that their polling place may have changed since the last time they voted and voters may spend more time at check-in securing needed information and slow the line down. High-stimulus elections lengthen lines due to high turnout while they may also slow the line down because there are more voters with less experience and information. Thus, the estimates we have made about wait times in the 2014 election err on the optimistic side if applied directly to predicting presidential elections.

The PCEA report outlines best practices for election administrators, giving specific attention to voter experiences including, but not limited to, poll wait times. Recognizing that long lines often occur because of a fundamental mismatch between the number of voters and the resources to accommodate them, the commission called for greater attention to polling-place congestion.

Addressing wait-time concerns is important because extended wait times tend to discourage voters, which may impact their willingness to vote or otherwise take part in other aspects of civic and political life. This look at Florida's wait-time experience in 2012 and Magnolia County's in 2014 speaks to the possibilities and limitations for improving wait times and enhancing voter confidence in elections. Magnolia County voters had one of the worst experiences with long lines in the state with the longest wait times in 2012. Through the measurement of service times at polling places in 2014, we see that the simple—but expensive—route of providing greater capacity to check in voters would go a long way toward making lines significantly shorter in Florida in future presidential elections and in high-profile midterm elections.

## NOTES

Part of the research reported in this chapter was supported by a generous grant from the Democracy Fund, which bears no responsibility for the findings reported here.

1. Barack Obama, "President Obama's Acceptance Speech," November 7, 2012.

2. Barack Obama, "Remarks by the President in the State of the Union Address," February 12, 2013.

3. Barack Obama: "Executive Order 13639—Establishment of the Presidential Commission on Election Administration," March 28, 2013. The Presidential Commission on Election Administration (PCEA) January 2014 report, "The American Voting Experience: Report and Recommendations of the Presidential Commission on Election Administration" may be found at http://web.mit.edu/supportthevoter/www/. Accessed 24 May 2017.

4. Uncontested races are left off the ballot.

5. This requirement speaks to a balancing issue related to ballot design. Many states schedule state and local elections to coincide with federal Election Day to enhance voter convenience so that voters will not need to vote every year or several times in the same year. Adding election contests to the ballot will lengthen it and thus lengthen the time needed to complete it.

6. See "Section 203 of the Voting Rights Act" available at http://www.justice.gov/crt/about/vot/sec_203/203_brochure.php. Accessed 24 May 24 2017.

7. Miami–Dade County Florida provides three ballot languages including English, Spanish, and Haitian Creole even though the percentage of Haitian Creole speakers,

at 4.2 percent, is less than the 5 percent minimum. Almost two-thirds of Miami–Dade County residents speak only Spanish at home.

8. See the National Council of State Legislatures at http://www.ncsl.org/research/elections-and-campaigns/voter-id.aspx#Details.

9. "How Long It Took Different Groups to Vote" (graphic), *New York Times*, February 4, 2013, available at http://www.nytimes.com/interactive/2013/02/05/us/politics/how-long-it-took-groups-to-vote.htm.

10. Exceptions include Highton (2006); Spencer and Markovits (2010); Allen and Bernshteyn (2013); Edelstein and Edelstein (2010); Olabisi and Chukwunoso (2012); Yang et al. (2014) and Buell (2013).

11. We honor a promise made to the county supervisor of elections to not divulge the county name in any research reports produced for public consumption.

12. US Census, State and County QuickFacts, available at https://www.census.gov/quickfacts/table/INC110215/12095,00. Accessed 24 May 2017.

13. US Census, State and County QuickFacts, available at https://factfinder.census.gov/faces/tableservices/jsf/pages/productview.xhtml?src=CF. Accessed 24 May 2017.

14. Information about PPOTF may be found at http://web.mit.edu/vtp. Accessed 24 May 2017.

15. Magnolia County has over two hundred precincts.

16. Florida allows several types of identification to be used to establish voter identity. Voters must produce a signature and photographic identification although identification sources need not be government issued. Both pieces of identification need not be from the same information source. Voters may produce one signature and one photo identification to vote in Florida.

17. The number of voters balking and opting not to vote (likely out of frustration) was also recorded.

18. Magnolia County uses electronic poll books resembling laptops on which voter information is stored.

19. The standard deviations of these means were: check-in time, 2:05; voting time, 4:11; scanning time, 11:02; and total time, 11:22 based on 297 (voting and scanning time) and 327 (check-in time) observations.

20. Little's Law is stated here as: where $L$ = the long-term average number of customers in a stable system, $\lambda$ = the long-term effective arrival rate, and $W$ = the average time a customer spends in the system. Rearranging terms, we can express the average wait time, $W$, as $L/\lambda$.

21. This result was calculated from the 2014 oversample study of one thousand Florida respondents. The standard error of this estimate is 0.9 minutes, which puts the 95 percent confidence interval of the statewide wait-time average at 7.3 $\pm$ 1.8 minutes. Looking at Magnolia County respondents alone, the average wait time among Election Day voters is 4.6 minutes. With the smaller sample size, the standard error is much larger, therefore, the 95 percent confidence interval for Magnolia County using the 2014 Survey of the Performance of American Elections is 4.6 $\pm$ 3.7 minutes, which encompasses the estimate made using Little's Law.

22. http://web.mit.edu/supportthevoter/www/. Accessed 24 May 2017. The tool is physically hosted at web.mit.edu/vtp/calc1.html. Accessed 24 May 2017.

23. Candidate names appearing at the top of the ballot are advantaged especially when voters have no other information about them (Matson and Fine 2006).

# Chapter 8

# Wait Times and Voter Confidence
## A Study of the 2014 Midterm Election in Miami-Dade County
*Michael C. Herron, Daniel A. Smith, Wendy Serra, and Joseph Bafumi*

"By the way, we have to fix that," President Obama *ad-libbed* during his victory speech on Election Night in 2012, responding to reports of excessive wait times at polling stations across the United States and particularly in Florida ("President Obama's Acceptance Speech," 2012). Acknowledging by name Desiline Victor, a 102-year-old Haitian American woman who waited in line nearly four hours at the North Miami Public Library early voting facility, the president emphasized in his 2013 State of the Union address that the electoral process in the United States "definitely needs improvement" as he announced the creation of a "nonpartisan commission to improve the voting experience in America" ("State of the Union 2013," 2013).

Whether out of a sense of urgency or shame, the state of Florida responded to the president's call. In the aftermath of the 2012 General Election, Florida Governor Rick Scott tasked his secretary of state, Ken Detzner, "to meet most immediately with those election supervisors who experienced lines in excess of four hours and those who took several days to tabulate votes and report results" (Turner 2014 39). In his ensuing report, Detzner (2013) acknowledged that "many voters found themselves waiting in line for hours to cast a ballot both during the early voting period and on Election Day," and that "most, if not all, counties experienced longer wait times than in previous elections due to factors including the record number of voters, a shortened early voting schedule, inadequate voting locations, limited voting equipment and a long ballot."

Despite Secretary Detzner's postelection report and the national concern over wait times, as Stewart (2013b, 445–47) observes, "the empirical study of waiting in line to vote is still in its infancy." Few scholars have investigated whether there are certain times during Election Day or certain stages in the voting process that are associated with extensive lines; even less is known about whether long lines have unsavory side effects such as causing voters to lose confidence in electoral processes.

With this as context, we explore the extent to which voter wait times fluctuated over the course of Election Day 2014 in ten precincts across Miami-Dade County, Florida, and whether certain voters were more likely than others to face a disproportionate "time tax" when waiting to cast their ballots (Mukherjee 2009). Additionally, we consider whether waiting in line creates concerns about ballot secrecy or leads voters to doubt that their votes will be counted as intended. Our results draw on voter check-in times recorded in electronic poll books and a set of exit polls that we conducted during the midterm election. Overall, our findings provide insight as to who is more likely to be confronted with disproportionately long wait times and whether wait times affect subsequent voter perceptions of electoral integrity.

### STUDYING WAIT TIMES

There are several reasons for the dearth of literature on voting lines and their consequences. First, it is often difficult, if not outright prohibited, to observe directly what transpires inside precincts. In Florida, for example, § Florida Statutes, chapter 102, section 031, subsection 4(a) requires that precinct observers must keep one hundred feet away from precinct entrances. If an observer cannot see beyond a physical precinct entrance, then she probably also cannot see how the lines may form. Second, it takes considerable resources to monitor voting processes in multiple polling stations. For example, in November 2014, there were nearly eight hundred

Election Day precincts in Miami-Dade County alone and thousands more precincts across Florida's other sixty-six counties. Third, it is difficult to hold constant across precincts a raft of factors that might lead to long voter wait times, such as a lack of voting machines and staff, problems with voter registration lists, different ballot lengths, and so forth.

Of the handful of studies that have examined the causes of long lines, most have leveraged observational data at the precinct level (Highton 2006; Allen and Bernshteyn 2006; Spencer and Markovits 2010; Herron and Smith 2015; Herron and Smith 2016). Other scholars have conducted surveys to study wait times and line formation, shedding light on whether some types of voters face disproportionately long lines (Alvarez et al. 2009; Pettigrew 2013; Stewart 2013a; and Kimball 2013). We, too, rely to a large extent on survey data, in this case, an exit poll of voters in Miami-Dade County in the 2014 Midterm Election. What is noteworthy about our poll, though, is that it combines questions about voting lines with specific questions about voter confidence, allowing us to assess the putative effect of waiting in line on voter perceptions of electoral transparency and fairness.

To the best of our knowledge, there are no existing studies that consider whether waiting at the polls has downstream consequences. We hypothesize that extensive waiting in line causes voters to lose confidence in electoral processes writ large; lines can be disorganized and their presence can be associated with malapportionment of resources and a general state of confusion. How might a confidence shock in the electoral processes manifest itself? This question is an important one, and we posit that a voter who loses confidence in the electoral process may doubt two of the most important practices in American elections, namely, ballot secrecy and accurate tabulating of votes. We thus operationalize confidence with two survey questions, one of which pertains to ballot secrecy and a second that asks voters about the likelihood of votes being counted as intended. In part, our interest in ballot secrecy is a response to research carried out by Gerber et al. (2013, 2014), who use a variety of methods to examine voters' psychological and social perceptions of ballot secrecy and have also examined whether doubts about voting secrecy depress turnout. They show that about a quarter of voters do not believe in ballot secrecy and that this impacts their vote choices.

While existing research on election administration does not connect wait times at the polls and voter perceptions of ballot secrecy, the idea that a bad experience at the polls may affect a voter's beliefs about electoral processes is not novel. For example, studies have shown that poll workers are evaluated less favorably when voters think their privacy may be compromised (Claassen et al. 2008); relatedly, racial and ethnic minorities are disproportionately less likely to think that their ballots are private (Karpowitz et al. 2011). We build on findings that connect voting experiences and voter perceptions by studying the consequences of a negative experience at the polls (i.e., being forced to wait to vote) with beliefs about election integrity.

## RESEARCH DESIGN

On Election Day, November 4, 2014, we administered exit polls at ten Miami-Dade County precincts. In order to assure a broad cross-section of voters in a county with nearly 1.4 million registered voters, we chose precincts that varied in race/ethnicity and had different histories of wait times. We had hoped to choose precincts based on a stratified random sample of the county's nine hundred precincts, but this approach ran into several difficulties. For example, precincts with multiple entrances were complicated for us since we had small teams of survey administrators at each precinct; we thus eliminated from consideration precincts with multiple entrances and exits. We also needed to ensure that we could access our chosen precincts during the day, and this imposed requirements on how the selected precincts were distributed across the county. Finally, for each of our chosen precincts we needed clearance from the Miami-Dade supervisor of elections (SOE). In Florida, elections are administered by independently elected county SOEs; all SOEs in Florida are elected, with the exception of Miami-Dade's, who is appointed by the governor.

We stationed a team of enumerators at each of our precincts. Voters were approached on Election Day as they exited the polls, and our pollsters attempted to give a survey to as many respondents as possible. Enumerators conducted surveys starting at 7:00 A.M., when polls opened, until after 7:00 P.M., when they closed. If a participant accepted our anonymous, nonpartisan survey, she was handed a clipboard with an exit poll attached and told to answer all questions to the best of her knowledge. We offered our surveys in English (see appendix 1), Spanish, and Haitian-Creole and received 508 completed or partially completed surveys.

Table 8.1 lists the ten precincts that we studied and provides the demographics of each precinct's Election Day voters and the number of surveys we gathered from each precinct. As the table shows, our ten precincts varied with respect to race/ethnicity; some precincts were majority Hispanic and others, majority black. The precincts were scattered across the county, and this ensures that results based on them do not reflect any idiosyncrasies associated with a particular location in Miami-Dade. According to the December 31, 2014, Florida statewide voter file, the registered voter pool in the county was approximately 19 percent black, 55 percent Hispanic, and 20 percent white.

**Table 8.1.** Ten Election Day Precincts in Miami-Dade County

| Precinct | Precinct | Voters | Black | Hispanic | White | Exit polls |
|----------|----------|--------|-------|----------|-------|------------|
| 113 | Point East Condominium | 289 | 3.81% | 46.71% | 44.46% | 21 |
| 146 | Keystone Park Community Center | 631 | 6.18% | 33.91% | 40.89% | 63 |
| 209 | Madie Ives Elementary School | 683 | 59.59% | 20.79% | 11.86% | 29 |
| 246 | Mt. Zion Apostolic Temple | 297 | 25.25% | 64.98% | 5.72% | 54 |
| 388 | West Hialeah Gardens Elementary School | 404 | 0.00% | 91.83% | 4.70% | 54 |
| 408 | Fontainebleau Milton Rental Apartments | 480 | 2.92% | 82.29% | 9.17% | 72 |
| 579 | Silver Bluff Elementary School | 619 | 1.29% | 73.67% | 20.68% | 48 |
| 640 | Bank UTD Center at University of Miami | 309 | 9.06% | 26.54% | 51.46% | 39 |
| 757 | Country Walk Park Recreation Center | 988 | 9.21% | 58.30% | 26.82% | 91 |
| 856 | Goulds Park | 487 | 88.71% | 6.78% | 0.82% | 37 |
| Total | | 5,187 | 21.30% | 50.07% | 23.02% | 508 |

Our survey includes questions asking voters when they arrived at the polls; with this question we calculated total voting times by subtracting arrival times from the times that the surveys were filled out. Our surveys also asked of each voter, "Approximately how long did you wait in line before checking in to vote?" For this question voters could choose from among the following: no wait at all; fewer than 10 minutes; between 10 and 30 minutes; between 31 and 60 minutes; between one and two hours; between three and four hours; and at least five hours. Lastly, the survey asked participants about the extent to which they thought their ballots were secret, and this question offered five answers: very confident; somewhat confident; not too confident; not at all confident; and do not know. A similar, five-option question was asked about confidence that one's vote would be counted as intended.

Not all survey respondents answered every question on our survey. As discussed later, we drop surveys that are missing answers to almost all pertinent questions, and we use multiple imputation where possible to impute missing values for survey questions on gender and on the extent to which a survey respondent said that voting lines affect when she votes. Beyond our survey, we characterize patterns in voter check-in times across our ten precincts for all 5,187 voters who cast ballots in them. Miami-Dade uses an Electronic Voter Identification (EViD) system, and this system records the official check-in times of all Election Day voters.

## FINDINGS

We begin with EViD data, which are described in figure 8.1. The top panel of this figure reports in ten-minute increments the number of voters who checked in at each of our precincts. The panel's loess smoother shows that greater numbers of voters checked in around 7:00 A.M., close to when the polls opened, and again later in the evening, close to when the polls closed at 7:00 P.M. It also reveals that there were a few dozen voters who checked in to vote *after* 7:00 P.M., indicating that they were in line (and thus permitted to vote) when the polls officially closed to new arrivals. The top panel of figure 8.1 comports with Spencer and Markovits's (2010) study of California arrival times, with higher rates of voters arriving at the polls in the early morning and later evening hours.

There was variability across our ten precincts both in total numbers of voters and when they checked in, and this is illustrated in the bottom panel of figure 8.1, which displays ten smoothers based on EViD data.

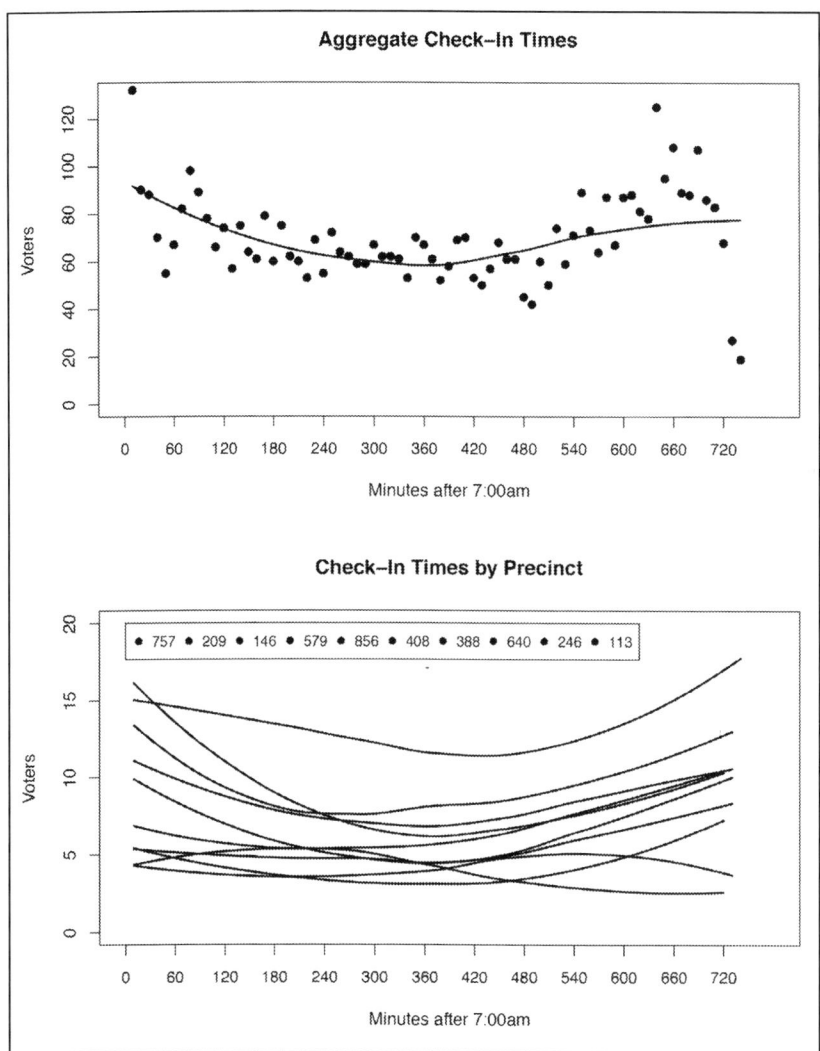

**Figure 8.1.** EViD Data from Ten Miami-Dade Precincts

There is one smoother per precinct, and each smoother in the panel is parameterized like the overall smoother in figure 8.1. Note that the bottom panel of figure 8.1 contains a legend that maps smoother color to precinct number, and precincts are sorted left to right by the number of voters that they processed on Election Day. Figure 8.1's bottom panel is useful because it displays the substantial variation in check-in times across our ten precincts. Precinct 757 was the busiest precinct of our ten, Precinct 209 was the second most active precinct, and Precinct 113 processed the fewest voters.

Patterns in the smoothers in figure 8.1's bottom panel show that most precincts had two peaks of voters, in the morning and early in the evening. This pattern did not hold for all precincts; the two most obvious exceptions to it are Precincts 640 and 113. The former, located on the campus of the University of Miami in Coral Gables, had a (relative) surge of voters around 5:00 P.M. and serviced relatively few voters in the morning; this conceivably reflects the voting habits of college students. The aforementioned Precinct 113, which had the lowest number of Election Day voters (289) of any of our polling stations, was located within a retirement complex and had a (relative) surge around 11:00 A.M., only to drop off the rest of the day. If one envisions that the typical post–5:00 P.M. surge in check-ins reflects the end of the standard workday, then we would expect this surge to be muted in precincts with large numbers of retirees.

EViD data describe check-in and not arrival times of voters, so to address the latter we turn to the exit polls described earlier. Our survey contained the question, "At what time did you arrive at the polls to vote today?" Fortuitously, nearly 83 percent of surveyed voters who were exiting the polls answered the question. At a few of the precincts we surveyed (Precincts 209, 757, and 856), several voters arrived well *before* the polls opened at 7:00 A.M., some as early as 6:00 A.M.

We next turn to the overall time a voter spent at the polls, and we measure this in minutes from the time a voter reported arriving at her precinct to the time she left the precinct and volunteered to take our exit poll. Overall, our exit polls show that the median overall time at the polls for the 361 voters who provided an arrival time and for whom our enumerators recorded the time of the exit poll was roughly 20 minutes, with an average value of nearly 25 minutes (s.d. = 8.4). Median values notwithstanding, there was considerable variation in wait times across our ten precincts. For example, voters in Precinct 757 reported the longest median overall time voting, roughly 32 minutes based on arrival to exit. Several Precinct 757 voters reported that they spent over an hour at their voting locations. Obviously, outliers like this might reflect voters who had long conversations (possibly unrelated to voting) in a precinct. In contrast, the median voter in Precinct 146 reported spending a total of only 14.5 minutes voting. Note that the time we are referring to here is encompassing—from arriving at the polls, waiting in line outside the polling station if necessary, checking in, receiving and filling out a ballot, scanning the ballot, and exiting the precinct—and thus is an overall voting experience time.

We have thus far offered evidence that there was variance within and across Miami-Dade precincts in terms of voter experience times. There is nothing inherently problematic with this; even if the precincts were similarly staffed and followed identical procedures, we would still not expect complete uniformity in voter experiences. Moreover, while our plots are illustrative, they cannot be used to draw conclusions about whether wait times for certain types of voters are disproportionately long (or short), conditional on a set of covariates.

With this in mind, we now present the results of estimating an ordered logistic regression ("ordered logit") that models voter self-reported wait times as a function of various individual level variables. The dependent variable in our logit model is the answer to the survey question, "Approximately how long did you wait in line before checking in to vote," and the survey allowed for seven answers; we disregard the sixth and seventh ("3–4 hours" and "5 hours or more," respectively) as no voters provided them. The five meaningful responses, the shortest of which was "not at all" and the longest "1–2 hours," are ordered; hence our use of an ordered logit model. In the analyses that follows we drop a small number of our surveys (thirteen) that are missing responses to almost every relevant survey question. Table 8.2 contains ordered logit estimates, and the model reflects data on 421 respondents; standard errors are clustered on precinct and the model includes precinct fixed effects. We use multiple imputation to impute values of gender when possible. More precisely, we impute gender using seven survey questions pertaining to wait time, whether a voter had registration problems, whether a voter faced equipment problems when voting, whether a voter used a ballot in a language other than English, whether a voter had previously voted at his or her precinct prior to November 2014, and whether a voter had children under the age of eighteen and at home. In addition, the survey allowed voters to choose from among seven race/ethnicity groups. However, we drop voters who chose "American Indian/Alaskan Native," "Asian/Pacific Islander," or "Other" because there were so few respondents (three, six, and nine, respectively) from these groups.

Table 8.2 reveals that white voters reported significantly shorter wait times when checking in to vote compared to black voters, the reference category in our logit model. This is consistent with literature that we have cited above, and this finding holds conditional on precinct fixed effects. We also find that voters who completed our survey in Spanish reported significantly less time waiting in line prior to checking in than those who responded in English, all else equal. It may be that predominantly Spanish language speakers who bother to vote are more engaged in the political process than the average English language speaker at the polls, enabling them to complete their ballot faster. We also find wealthier voters (those with a household income greater than $100,000) reported disproportionately shorter wait times than their less wealthy counterparts. Older voters reported waiting in line longer than younger voters before being processed. While this may point to slower tendencies of older voters, it just as likely reflects the fact that they arrive at the polls in clusters as suggested in figure 8.1.

**Table 8.2.** Self-Reported Wait Times Prior to Checking In to Vote

| Variable | Wait time |
| --- | --- |
| Hispanic | -0.441 |
| | (0.344) |
| White | -1.200*** |
| | (0.463) |
| Multiracial | -0.495 |
| | (0.636) |
| Spanish | -0.971** |
| | (0.494) |
| Male | 0.112 |
| | (0.250) |
| Republican | 0.0648 |
| | (0.277) |
| No Party Affiliation (NPA) | 0.461 |
| | (0.281) |
| Household income > $100,000 | -0.408** |
| | (0.206) |

| Variable | Wait time |
|---|---|
| Age | 0.0244*** |
|  | (0.00595) |
| Voted at polling station before (1=No) | 0.105 |
|  | (0.242) |
| Some college or more | 0.0684 |
|  | (0.247) |
| Observations | 421 |

Note: *** p<0.01, ** p<0.05, * p<0.1; precinct fixed effects not shown.

All ten of our precincts were located in urban parts of Miami-Dade County. The fact that across these precincts there was not only considerable variation across precincts in self-reported voter wait times but also across demographic groups suggests that studies on wait times that use less-refined measures of where a precinct is located—such as a county or a ZIP code—may understate the extent of variance in voter experiences. As is clear from our exit polls, even in a relatively low turnout election voters in a single election administrative jurisdiction experienced vastly different wait times on Election Day.

We now consider the consequences of wait times for voter confidence. Recall that our exit poll asked voters whether they are very confident, somewhat confident, not too confident, or not at all confident that their votes will be kept secret. Using the same set of ordered categories, our survey also measured voter confidence that one's vote will count as intended. Our survey allowed respondents to answer "Don't know" to the questions on ballot secrecy and counting, and we drop from our analyses respondents who gave these answers. We analyze what predicts responses to these questions using two ordered logit models, and the predictors in these models include our categorical wait-time variable as well as a battery of control variables. As in previous models, our two ordered logit models use multiple imputation of gender and whether a voter believes that line length affects when she votes.

Table 8.3 presents the results of two ordered logit models, the first of which has as its dependent variable a voter's perception of ballot secrecy and the second, a voter's confidence that her vote will be counted as intended. Our primary interest is whether disproportionate wait times at the polls are reflected in perceptions voters have about electoral processes, and table 8.3 shows that, compared to voters who had no wait at all prior to checking in to vote, voters who had the longest reported wait times had less confidence that their ballots would be kept secret and their votes were accurately tabulated. This finding highlights how bad experiences at the polls (and here we assume that long waits are experiences of this type) may have downstream effects on voters. Of course, our data cannot speak to whether the negative confidence shocks we see in table 8.3 are transient or enduring.

Beyond the consequences of wait times, table 8.3 shows that all racial groups have greater confidence in the secrecy of their vote compared to black voters, the reference category. Moreover, we see that older voters have more confidence in ballot secrecy than younger voters. We do not find any evidence of partisanship on ballot secrecy, nor do we find income or education effects. It bears noting that Gerber et al. (2013) find that education predicts feelings of psychological secrecy; they do not find any evidence of race effects, though, and they only include demographic covariates in their model, whereas we include partisanship and other controls. Nonetheless, because we controlled for partisanship and income in table 8.3, we need not be overly concerned that, say, voters of a certain political party, many of whom doubt the institution of ballot secrecy, arrived at the polls at idiosyncratic times, all of which had long lines. Lastly, voters who did not have any problems with voting equipment and voters who did not have to update their addresses were significantly more likely to have confidence in the secrecy of their ballots.

**Table 8.3.** Voter Perceptions of Ballot Secrecy and Intended Tabulating

| Variable | Vote secret | Vote counted |
|---|---|---|
| Cast a provisional ballot (1=No) | 0.685 | 0.262 |
| | (0.806) | (0.682) |
| Waited less than 10 minutes | 0.414 | 0.111 |
| | (0.460) | (0.332) |
| Waited 10-30 minutes | 0.248 | -0.0179 |
| | (0.532) | (0.485) |
| Waited 31-60 minutes | 1.072*** | 0.503** |
| | (0.272) | (0.219) |
| Problem with registration (1=No) | -1.349 | -0.670 |
| | (1.334) | (1.103) |
| Problem with voting equipment (1=No) | -14.18*** | 0.609 |
| | (1.079) | (0.901) |

| Variable | Vote secret | Vote counted |
|---|---|---|
| Hispanic | -2.127*** | -0.888* |
| | (0.668) | (0.534) |
| White | -1.446*** | 0.0527 |
| | (0.535) | (0.710) |
| Multiracial | -2.950*** | -0.558 |
| | (0.744) | (0.608) |
| Exit poll conducted in Spanish | -0.0279 | -0.229 |
| | (0.266) | (0.513) |
| Male | 0.630* | 0.241 |
| | (0.364) | (0.242) |
| Line length affects when voting (1=No) | -0.251 | 0.123 |
| | (0.290) | (0.280) |
| Republican | 0.404 | 0.0983 |
| | (0.565) | (0.495) |
| No Party Affiliation (NPA) | 0.628 | 0.558 |
| | (0.952) | (0.458) |
| Household income > $100,000 | -0.501 | -0.323 |
| | (0.357) | (0.205) |
| Age | -0.0198** | -0.0294*** |
| | (0.00819) | (0.00988) |
| Updated address at polls (1=No) | -1.055** | -0.873* |
| | (0.538) | (0.530) |
| Brought sample ballot to polls (1=No) | -0.179 | 0.142 |
| | (0.575) | (0.373) |
| Prior vote at polling station (1=No) | 0.0947 | 0.375* |
| | (0.242) | (0.208) |
| Some college or more | -0.141 | 0.413 |
| | (0.383) | (0.417) |
| Observations | 394 | 390 |

Note: *** p<0.01, ** p<0.05, * p<0.1; precinct fixed effects not shown.

With respect to the second model in table 8.3, we also find that older voters are more confident than their younger counterparts that their votes will be counted properly. This is similar to what we found regarding ballot secrecy above. We can only speculate as to the origins of these findings; perhaps younger voters are more prone to conspiracy theories about stolen elections given the 2000 presidential election and the increased scrutiny the voting process has undergone since then. Notably, we find no evidence of race/ethnicity or partisan effects on perceptions of accurate vote tabulation.

Two caveats about table 8.3 are important. First, our findings about ballot secrecy and confidence in vote tabulation are conditional on turnout, and this means that we cannot describe perceptions of ballot secrecy and accurate tabulation for nonvoters. Second, since we did not assign wait times randomly, we cannot be sure that we have found a causal relationship between wait times and voter perceptions. Nonetheless, a reverse causality story seems somewhat hard to maintain. For example, might the most diffident voters tend to vote in packs, thus inducing long lines and a spurious relationship between confidence and wait times? While in principle this is possible, we cannot think of a good theoretical reason for this type of coordination.

CONCLUSION

Wait times at the polls were flagged by President Obama in his State of the Union address following the 2012 General Election, and the seeming persistence of long lines to vote were subsequently highlighted in a report authored by the Presidential Commission on Election Administration. In light of the prominence of voting lines, this mixed-methods study is among the first to delve into the matters of who is more likely to wait in line and for how long and whether facing long lines at the polls may cloud voters' perceptions about the integrity of the voting process itself.

Drawing on electronic poll book check-in times and more than five hundred exit polls, we find evidence that white voters reported shorter wait times than black voters and that younger and wealthier voters spent less time at the polls than older and poorer voters. We also find that voters who waited more than half an hour in line before checking in to vote reported less confidence in the secrecy of their votes than voters who reported no wait time. Black voters, younger voters, voters who had problems with the voting equipment, and voters who had to update their addresses also exhibited less confidence in this way. And with regard to perceptions of whether ballots would be accurately counted, we find that younger voters and those who waited a disproportionate amount of time to check in to vote similarly reported having less confidence that their votes would be counted properly.

Election administrators in Florida and beyond face a complicated task in their efforts to make the voting experience as smooth, efficient, and secure as possible. Fortuitously, the median wait time in the ten Miami-Dade precincts we studied satisfies the recommendation of the Presidential Commission on Election Administration that "local officials should be able to plan the allocation of their resources such that during the normal course of the day, nearly all voters can be processed within the 30-minute standard" (Persily 2014). Our findings, however, that voters who experience long lines may be disproportionately skeptical that their votes will be kept secret or will be counted should be a concern to all local election administrators. Perhaps more voter education about voting processes, emphasizing that the experience of facing longer lines at the polls does not necessarily bear any relationship to other facets of voting like ballot secrecy, might be needed. Most importantly, however, voting processes should continue to be reformed so that voting is conducted efficiently. Our results suggest that this will give voters more confidence in the electoral process writ large.

## ACKNOWLEDGMENTS

This study was approved by the Committee for the Protection of Human Subjects at Dartmouth College (STUDY00028440) and the Institutional Review Board at the University of Florida (2014-U-1204). The authors thank Penelope Townsley, former Miami-Dade County Supervisor of Elections Christina White, and other staff for their generous assistance and for providing us with EViD data from the 2014 Midterm Election. The authors also thank Micole Kaye and the many research assistants who helped Herron and Smith conduct the surveys. Herron thanks the Office of the Dean of the Faculty at Dartmouth College for the Scholarly Innovation and Advancement Award that funded the survey used here. The authors thank Charles Stewart III for his helpful comments.

## APPENDIX 1: EXIT POLL

| Precinct | Dartmouth College (CPHS #28440)<br>Univ. of Florida (IRB #2014-U-1204 | Time | YOUR ANSWERS ARE **CONFIDENTIAL**<br>Please check only ONE response for each question. |

[A] Gender
1.☐ Male        2.☐ Female

[B] Race/Ethnicity
1.☐ American Indian/Alaskan Native
2.☐ Asian/Pacific Islander
3.☐ Black, *not of* Hispanic origin
4.☐ Hispanic
5.☐ White, *not of* Hispanic origin
6.☐ Multi-racial
7.☐ Other

[C] At what time did you arrive at the polls to vote today?
_____   ☐ A.M. ☐ P.M.

[D] Does line length affect what time of day you vote?
1.☐ Yes        2.☐ No

[E] Did you try to vote earlier today?
1.☐ Yes        2.☐ No

[F] How did you get to the polls today?
1.☐ Walked
2.☐ Drove Self
3.☐ Driven by Someone Else
4.☐ Bus or public transportation
5.☐ Bicycle
6.☐ Other

[G] Did you come to vote alone or with someone else?
1.☐ Alone        2.☐ With someone else

[H] Approximately how long did you wait in line before checking in to vote?
1.☐ Not at all
2.☐ Less than 10 minutes
3.☐ 10-30 minutes
4.☐ 31 minutes to 60 minutes
5.☐ 1-2 hours
6.☐ 3-4 hours
7.☐ 5 hours or more

[I] Did you use a driver's license as your form of photo ID?
1.☐ Yes        2.☐ No

[J] Was there a problem with your voter registration when you tried to vote?
1.☐ Yes        2.☐ No

[K] Did you have to vote a "provisional ballot" today?
1.☐ Yes        2.☐ No

[L] How confident are you that your vote will be counted as you intended?
1.☐ Very confident     4.☐ Not at all confident
2.☐ Somewhat confident  5.☐ I don't know
3.☐ Not too confident

[M] How confident are you that your vote was secret?
1.☐ Very confident     4.☐ Not at all confident
2.☐ Somewhat confident  5.☐ I don't know
3.☐ Not too confident

[N] Did you encounter any problems with the voting equipment or the ballot that may have interfered with your ability to cast your vote as intended?
1.☐ Yes        2.☐ No
If Yes, please specify what problem, or problems, you had:_____

[O] Did you bring a sample ballot with you into the polling booth to assist you in filling out your ballot?
1.☐ Yes        2.☐ No

[P] No matter how you voted today, with which party are you registered?
1.☐ Florida Democratic Party
2.☐ Republican Party of Florida
3.☐ No Party Affiliation (NPA)
4.☐ Other
5.☐ Don't know

[Q] In what year did you register to vote in Florida?
_____

[R] Was this your first time voting in Miami-Dade County?
1.☐ Yes        2.☐ No

[S] Did you update your address when you voted today?
1.☐ Yes        2.☐ No

[T] Have you ever voted at this polling station before?
1.☐ Yes        2.☐ No

[U] During which stage of the voting process did you spend the most time?
1.☐ Joining the line before checking in to vote.
2.☐ Checking in to vote.
3.☐ Filling out the ballot.
4.☐ Scanning the ballot.

[V] Did you have any difficulty understanding the ballot?
1.☐ Yes        2.☐ No

[W] What was the last grade of school you completed?
1.☐ Did not complete high school
2.☐ High school graduate
3.☐ Some college or associate's degree
4.☐ College graduate
5.☐ Post-graduate study

[X] How old are you? _____

[Y] Do you have any children under the age of 18 at home?
1.☐ Yes        2.☐ No

[Z] Employment status:
1.☐ Working now
2.☐ Temporarily laid off
3.☐ Unemployed
4.☐ Retired
5.☐ Permanently Disabled
6.☐ Homemaker
7.☐ Student

[ZZ] Total Household Income in 2013
1.☐ Under $15,000          5.☐ $75,000-$99,999
2.☐ $15,000-$29,999        6.☐ $100,000-$149,999
3.☐ $30,000-$49,999        7.☐ $150,000-$199,999
4.☐ $50,000-$74,999        8.☐ $200,000 or more

# Policy

# Chapter 9

# The Affordable Care Act and the Outcome of the 2014 US Senate Elections

*Sean D. Foreman*

In every election it is our political instinct to look for the common themes or set of issues that were the most important topics for shaping voting behavior. In 1994 the Contract for America was a galvanizing force for Republicans and in 2006 opposition to the war in Iraq fueled Democratic gains in Congress. The passage in March 2010 of the Patient Protection and Affordable Care Act (ACA) made healthcare reform a hot political topic in 2010. By 2014 the ACA, or Obamacare as it is commonly called, continued to be a heated issue. The healthcare reform law was a focal point for both political parties in the 2012 General Election, even with the Supreme Court ruling upholding the law that June. As Obamacare provisions went into full effect by 2014, and as states continued to challenge the law, it was expected that healthcare reform would be a major campaign issue in the 2014 Midterm Elections. Public opinion on the ACA favored Republicans approaching Obama's second midterm election.

The question asked in this chapter is, did voter attitudes about the ACA impact vote choice and electoral outcomes in the 2014 US Senate campaigns? Conventional wisdom held that the ACA would have an electoral influence on the 2014 congressional races. Through an examination of polls, media coverage, advertisements, and candidate platforms, the impact of Obamacare on key Senate races is examined in five southern states (Arkansas, Georgia, Kentucky, Louisiana, and North Carolina) plus Alaska and Iowa. The ACA was a significant issue for discussion in these campaigns, in that it was a focus in campaign ads and was asked about in polls, but it was not the determining issue that drove voter action.

In 2013–14 perceptions about the president's handling of the economy was a major issue for voters. Beyond that, healthcare, entitlement reform, immigration, and foreign policy were other issues that were in the headlines and on the electorate's minds.

The first major electoral impact of the ACA was its role in the rise of Tea Party candidates in the 2010 elections. The March 2010 victory for Obama and the Democrats with a healthcare law passed in a partisan vote fueled conservative opposition to it in the 2010 Midterm Election. The modern Tea Party movement sparked simultaneously in early 2010 and culminated in a sweeping Republican victory with sixty-three additional seats and a House majority and a pickup of six seats in the Senate. With the majority Republican House they proceeded to vote multiple times to repeal the ACA even though there was no chance that the Democrat majority Senate would take up the legislation—let alone approve it—not to mention that President Obama would veto it. The ACA did not damage Obama much in his 2012 reelection campaign and he even embraced the name Obamacare in a debate with Mitt Romney.

Not only were there political attempts to repeal ACA but there were also legal battles. A joint lawsuit brought by twenty-six states sued the federal government over the individual mandate provision that required people to have health insurance or face a tax penalty on their income tax return. The states' case was consolidated with the case of the *National Federation of Independent Business v. Sebelius* (Secretary of Health and Human Services Kathleen Sebelius). In June 2012 the Court upheld the law and the individual mandate at the heart of it by a 5-4 decision. Chief Justice John Roberts delivered the swing vote and wrote the majority opinion to the chagrin of conservatives. With the decision, proponents of the ACA claimed it to be the "law of the land" and considered it a settled legal issue. Opponents determined to double down on their efforts to repeal and replace the healthcare law. The path to do that required Republicans to keep control of the House and to capture the Senate majority—and then win the presidency in 2016. The crucial step in the equation in 2014 was the focus on the Senate.

The ACA also played a prominent role in the Florida 13th congressional district special election in March 2014. In October 2013 Congressman Bill Young, a twenty-two-term incumbent, died (Meacham 2013). The race to succeed him was viewed as a harbinger of the 2014 midterms and as a test run for the effectiveness of campaigning against the ACA in November (Everett and Sherman, 2014; Fox 2014).

David Jolly, a lobbyist and former congressional staffer for Young, won a competitive Republican primary. Democratic party leaders cleared the field for former state CFO and 2010 gubernatorial nominee Alex Sink. Sink was a former bank executive with no Washington experience. Yet Jolly and outside groups ran ads tying Sink to Obamacare and criticizing her for supporting a law that cost more than two million jobs in Florida (Bergerson and Banyon 2015). Sink was tepid in her defense of the signature Democratic law and talked about fixing it but not repealing it.

Jolly defeated Sink by 3,494 votes (48.5 to 46.6 percent) despite both her early and late leads in the polls. Two issues stood out in polls as most important for voters: President Obama's popularity and the Affordable Care Act. The Jolly campaign downplayed the importance of Obamacare in deciding the election but Sink thought that the "nonstop negative ads" from Republicans and conservative groups was "obviously a factor" in the outcome (Krueger 2014).

## PUBLIC OPINION POLLS

The preponderance of polls asking voters' opinions about the Affordable Care Act found majority disapproval of the law leading up to the 2014 Midterm Election (McCarthy 2014a). A poll released right after the 2012 General Election on November 6–9 showed 37 percent approved and 56 percent disapproved while 6 percent expressed no opinion. After a handful of favorable polls in the three months after the law was passed, for the next several years more than 90 percent of the polls found more people were against the law than in favor of it (Real Clear Politics 2014). Most of all, Obamacare became, for the Republicans, an issue they could use for political purposes to exploit and exaggerate its results to gain favor with the electorate. Their cause was aided when President Obama's oft-repeated phrase "If you like your health care plan, you can keep it" was found to be the 2013 "lie of the year" by Politifact (Holan 2013).

In April Americans for Prosperity (AFP) started running ads against Democrats who had voted for Obamacare. "We do want to make sure that Obamacare is the number one issue in the country," said AFP President Tim Phillips (Fuller 2014). Congressional Republicans did their part to keep it in the news. The word "Obamacare" was mentioned 293 times in floor speeches in March 2014 while "unemployment" was only uttered forty-two times. Barack Obama was not on the ballot but he said that his policies were. Healthcare and the economy were often talked about in the battleground states. This was fueled by both individual Republican candidates who used it as an issue and by outside groups funded by super PACs running independent ads tying candidates like Mark Begich in Alaska and Mary Landrieu in Louisiana to Obama and Obamacare. In November 2013 the Republican National Committee used a robocall and Facebook postings urging people to call their members of Congress and ask "why they supported President Obama's lie" that people who wanted to keep their health care plan could under the ACA reforms. Among the eleven Democrats targeted were candidates for the Senate from Arkansas, Iowa, Louisiana, and North Carolina (OnTheIssues.org).

While most Democrats tried to distance themselves from the law, Republicans were largely on the offense about it. The Republican challengers each called their Democratic incumbent opponents the "deciding vote" on Obamacare and all proclaimed that they would vote to repeal the ACA. The problematic issues with the rollout of the website in October 2013 spelled disaster in the polls against the approval of the president and Democrats. That was another indicator that Obamacare would be discussed often and used in attack ads in the 2014 campaigns. When the ACA reenrollment period arrived, President Obama delayed the registration process until after the November election to avoid additional problems.

One way to determine the role healthcare played in voters' minds is by asking them in exit polls. From these polls we find that healthcare was an important issue to a significant number of voters but it was not an overwhelming factor. The opinions on healthcare probably overlapped with opinions on President Obama's job approval. In the 2014 national exit poll there were two questions on healthcare. One asked whether the respondent thought the ACA law went far enough, was about right, or went too far (see table 9.1).

The next question asked voters to identify the most important issue to them in the 2014 campaign. Alaska (27 percent) had the highest portion of voters saying that the law did not go far enough. They were followed by Kentucky (26 percent), North Carolina (25 percent), Georgia (24 percent), and Iowa. In each of these states, Republicans won by these respective margins: Alaska (3.2 percent), Kentucky (15.5 percent), North Carolina (1.7 percent), Iowa (8.5 percent), and Georgia (7.9 percent).

Of the states where people said it went too far, the least was in Kentucky (46 percent) and North Carolina (47 percent). The national average was that 49 percent thought it went too far. Iowa (50 percent), Alaska (51 percent), Georgia (51 percent), Arkansas (55 percent), and Louisiana (56 percent) had higher percentages who thought that the ACA went too far. Voters who thought the ACA was "about right," voted in high percentages for the Democratic candidates (ex. Landrieu 84 percent and Hagan 80 percent).

A view of the dynamics in each of these states' Senate campaigns will put a better perspective on the role that Obamacare played in voters' minds and what impact the law may have had on the 2014 Midterm Election outcomes.

**Table 9.1.** Percentage of Voters Who Thought Affordable Care Act

| State | Not far enough | About right | Went too far |
|---|---|---|---|
| Alaska | 27 | 17 | 51 |
| Arkansas | 16 | 21 | 55 |
| Georgia | 24 | 19 | 51 |
| Iowa | 24 | 19 | 50 |
| Kentucky | 26 | 22 | 46 |
| Louisiana | 19 | 20 | 56 |
| North Carolina | 25 | 22 | 47 |
| Nationally | 25 | 21 | 49 |

Source: CNN Exit Polls, accessed March 14, 2015, http://www.cnn.com/election/2014/results/exit-polls

## THE 2014 SENATE CAMPAIGN CASES

Seven US Senate races from competitive campaigns—five in the Deep South (Arkansas, Georgia, Kentucky, Louisiana, and North Carolina) plus Iowa and Alaska—demonstrate the impact of the ACA. Each of these states was rated as "toss-up" contests by The Cook Political Report (2014) through Election Day. These states, with the exception of Georgia and Kentucky, were held by vulnerable Democrats. Initially, Democrats thought they had a realistic chance to win both Georgia and Kentucky in 2014. Ultimately, Republicans won the majority with these five pick-ups and two holds.

*Alaska: Sullivan/Begich*

Mark Begich was one of the most vulnerable Democrats on the 2014 election map. Begich had the challenge of being a Democrat in a state with strong Republican advantages.

Dan Sullivan tagged Begich as the "deciding vote" on Obamacare, ultimately defeating Begich (McBeath and Shepro 2015). Begich was torn between being too close to the president and the ACA and trying to establish his independence from national Democrats. In the first debate, Begich claimed 37 percent of Alaskans were helped by the ACA, but overall did little to defend the healthcare law or his vote. Sullivan piled President Obama and Majority Leader Reid on top of Begich in his rhetorical attacks, which resonated with Alaskan voters.

Even before Sullivan won the primary, Republican groups put $10 million into the race, buying advertising that tied Begich to Obama and Obamacare. Begich called himself a "thorn" in the president's backside and said that Democrats and the president did not appreciate his independent streak (Fahrenthold 2014). The advertisements highlighted that Begich voted with Obama 97 percent of the time. Begich would emphasize that he had voted with fellow Alaska Senator Lisa Murkowski 80 percent of the time.

Sullivan enjoyed the Republican wave and the natural state advantage to defeat Begich 48 to 46 percent. Obamacare may have been a factor in Begich's loss but was certainly not the only one. Republican registered voters (136,645) outnumber Democrats (70,853) by nearly two to one, though Undeclared (190,307) and Nonpartisan (88,035) outnumber both of them. Begich had slight advantages on some local issues like union support and favorable ballot initiatives. Views on the president's job approval and the economy polled higher than concerns over healthcare law as factors driving voters.

*Arkansas: Cotton/Pryor*

Incumbent Democrat Mark Pryor faced mission impossible in running for his third term in the Senate. Pryor ran against the headwinds of the national anti-Democrat mood as well as trends against Democrats in Arkansas where his family is prominent in Democratic politics. Pryor's opponent, Republican Congressman Tom Cotton, was ready to fight for the Senate seat and tied Pryor to Obama and Obamacare as much as possible. Americans for Prosperity ran an ad highlighting Pryor's position on Obamacare starting in April. The super PAC, financially backed by the Koch Brothers, announced that they planned to spend more than $18 million in Arkansas throughout the course of the race (Saenz 2014).

Pryor released an ad in which he touted certain aspects of the healthcare law, but did not mention the law by name. Cotton admitted that his parents had been conservative Democrats who voted for Pryor and his father, David, a former governor and senator, "but like so many Arkansans, they realized that Barack Obama and Obama Democrats don't reflect the old conservative Democrats that they knew and grew up with." Cotton and outside groups were successful in tying Pryor to the president. "But distaste for Obama is particularly pronounced in Arkansas, where analysts and voters alike have traced the state's rightward turn to his election in 2008" (Huey-Burns 2014).

Pryor was the only Democrat in the state's congressional delegation. On the other hand, Cotton was the only one from the state to vote against the farm bill. Pryor ultimately was trounced on Election Day and in retrospect it seems like it was impossible for him to ever win the race even with all the outside support possible.

*Georgia: Perdue/Nunn*

In 2014 Georgia had an open seat with the retirement of Saxby Chambliss. The Republican-held seat was one where Democrats thought they might have a chance to compete with their nominee, Michelle Nunn, the daughter of former moderate Democrat Senator Sam Nunn (Zipperer 2013). The Republican nominee was David Perdue, a cousin of the former governor. There was also a Libertarian candidate, Amanda Swafford, who polled in single digits. But as the race between Perdue and Nunn was close and Georgia requires a Senate candidate to get more than 50 percent of the vote to avoid a runoff, Swafford's support was monitored.

An October 31 NBC News/Marist Poll (2014) showed that healthcare was the third most important issue to registered voters. Job creation and economic growth (27 percent) and Washington gridlock (16 percent) were the top two. In fourth place was Social Security and Medicare (13 percent). That poll found Perdue ahead of Nunn by 48-44 percent with 3 percent for the Libertarian candidate and 4 percent undecided. Nunn was not able to compete on money or message. She refused to embrace the Democratic Party or say whether she voted for the president. The opinions of Georgians on the ACA were at the median among the case studies. Perdue won by eight points.

### Iowa: Ernst/Braley

Five-term Senator Tom Harkin retired leaving an open seat in 2014. Congressman Bruce Braley, the Democratic nominee, was no Tom Harkin. Braley made several gaffes along the campaign trail and could not shake the support he previously showed for the ACA as a member of the House. Braley's opponent was Joni Ernst, not Taylor Swift. "I don't care if she's as good looking as Taylor Swift or as nice as Mr. Rogers, but if she votes like Michele Bachmann, she's wrong for the state of Iowa," Harkin quipped on the campaign trail (Glueck 2014).

Braley was an active supporter of the ACA as a House member and then even early in his Senate run. Braley said the House Republican votes in attempting to repeal Obamacare were "almost shocking" and he defended the law in a series of interviews. Braley, in his 2012 reelection campaign, was a "full throated" supporter of the ACA. His opponent tried to use it against him in calling for a repeal of Obamacare, but Iowa's 1st Congressional District is more liberal and voted in support of Obama. Still, his defense of the law in his 2012 district campaign was used against him in the 2014 Senate race (Noble 2012).

Braley was one of two Democrats in the House who voted for a proposed fix to Obamacare, a bill that was strongly opposed by the Obama

Administration.[1] But Braley could never run from the statement he made shortly after the March 2010 vote on the bill: "After reading the bill, listening to my constituents and debating the bill's provisions in Congress, I'm convinced this legislation is good for Iowa" (GOP 2013).

Ernst ran a snazzy ad that mentioned castrating hogs, and ran a simple and focused campaign against Obama's policies. That steadiness of message, combined with missteps by Braley and Harkin, led to an easy win for Ernst. After the election, Harkin speculated that the ACA was too complicated and that Democrats had fumbled the issue. "So I look back and say we should have either done it the correct way or not done anything at all," Harkin said (Bolton 2014). Polls on this race did not focus questions on the ACA, making it difficult to determine the actual role it played with Iowa voters.

### Kentucky: McConnell/Lundergan Grimes

Senator Mitch McConnell held one of the lone Republican seats that Democrats felt they had a chance to capture in 2014. While McConnell was a five-term senator and poised to be the majority leader should Republicans win majority control of the Senate, he was viewed as a boring, technocratic politician who was vulnerable to attack by outside groups on a host of positions he had taken over the years. Democrats nominated the secretary of state, Allison Lundergan Grimes. Grimes was a hometown girl from a political family. Her father, Jerry Lundergan, served in the Kentucky House of Representatives and as the chair of the Kentucky Democratic Party, and was a friend of former president Bill Clinton. Grimes, a promising, telegenic, thirty-five-year-old candidate, gained national attention, but she failed to dent McConnell's frontrunner status as he ran a steady campaign.

Grimes got caught up in an awkward moment in early October. She was asked by the *Louisville Courier-Journal* if she had voted for President Obama. She dodged and refused to give a direct answer. It was consistent with the message that Democrats were trying to convey—that they would not be tied to the president. In Kentucky, a state Obama twice lost, the president was particularly unpopular (Bump 2014).

A high percentage of Kentucky residents disapproved of Obamacare. But their opinions were positive for Kynect, the state healthcare exchange established under the Affordable Care Act. And while many people in

Kentucky benefited from the expansion of subsidized healthcare coverage, they were not seeking to reward Democrats for it. Grimes, who did not have a vote on the law, distanced herself from the president but not as much from the ACA. Grimes publicly supported Kentucky's expansion of Medicaid and argued for reforms to try to find fraud and reduce waste in the healthcare system.

Coal and energy policy seemed to be the most important issues for Kentucky voters. Still, healthcare was a winner for McConnell on the campaign trail. McConnell claimed that tens of thousands of Kentucky workers lost their health insurance plans under Obamacare and opposed the use of Medicare funds to pay for Obamacare. McConnell's contribution to the debate was that he wanted to see the ACA repealed and replaced with "common-sense reforms that would lower costs for Americans" (Stein 2014).

### Louisiana: Landrieu/Cassidy

Mary Landrieu, despite her family's success in Louisiana politics, was in for a tough battle in 2014. One hope for her was Louisiana's jungle primary in which candidates from all parties compete in a single primary election. If no candidate wins a majority of the vote, the top two vote-getters advance to a second-round runoff election. With several Republicans in the race, it would be difficult for the GOP favorite, US Representative Bill Cassidy, to win outright, presenting a slim chance for Landrieu to try to capture a majority in the first round. As the campaign progressed, however, it became clear that Landrieu would not be able to win in the primary and that Cassidy had a stronger than expected chance of winning in the first round to avoid the runoff.

The ACA was a dominant issue in the Pelican State's campaign. Louisiana had a higher (18 percent) than national average (15.8 percent) of uninsured residents. Combined with a high unemployment rate and a shrinking state budget, this made support for funding from Obamacare crucial for many of the state's residents. Landrieu, with an eye on her path to reelection in 2014, did vote for the ACA in 2009 and 2010 but only after securing an enticement of $300 million to fix the Federal Medical Assistance Percentages (FMAP) program in Louisiana (Stockley 2015). The deal was derisively dubbed the "Louisiana Purchase" and, while a similar deal was initially awarded to Nebraska (called the "Cornhusker Kick-back"), the Nebraska senator backed off from the arrangement after negative publicity. Landrieu did not.

When Louisiana's insurance commissioner announced that 93,000 Louisiana residents would lose their health insurance, and the website where people could sign up for a plan crashed, the ACA looked like a losing proposition for Landrieu (Deslatte 2013). Polls showed that a majority of Louisianans did not support the law overall but they did support components of it such as Medicaid expansion. But Governor Bobby Jindal blocked Medicaid expansion in the state. So Landrieu tempered her position, saying that she was for Medicaid expansion and also supported a legislative fix for those who lost their plan (Bash 2013; Goidel 2014; Jaffe 2013). Still, Landrieu said on the campaign trail, "If I had to vote for the bill again, I would vote for it tomorrow"; her statement along with the president's "lie of the year" were used in ads against her. Several polls in 2013 showed Landrieu ahead of Cassidy. In early 2014 Cassidy had pulled even with her. By the summer Cassidy was leading in the polls. The attacks based on Landrieu's support of the ACA seemed to work against her. Ultimately, Cassidy won the runoff by 56-44 percent.

## North Carolina: Hagan/Tillis

Kay Hagan also appeared to have an uphill battle in North Carolina to save her seat. Hagan was elected in 2008 as Barack Obama won North Carolina's presidential vote. Hagan was also considered to be vulnerable for having been a deciding vote on the ACA and having a voting record quite consistent with the president's agenda. Hagan's opponent was Thom Tillis, a former speaker of the North Carolina State House. Tillis won a spirited primary against a Tea Party–backed opponent amid charges that he was a RINO (Republican in name only) from the more conservative base. Some backers of Tillis's primary opponent were concerned that Tillis would moderate his stance on the ACA for the general election (Ball 2014; Maloy 2014).

Tillis made opposition to Medicaid expansion in North Carolina a signature position of his public service. And he campaigned for the Senate by bashing the ACA at every turn. On Tillis's campaign website he called the ACA "a cancer on our national economy." He voted to defund the law in what led to a government shutdown in October 2013. Tillis stated, "I believe Obamacare is a mortal threat to our economy. It will decrease healthcare quality and raise healthcare premiums and Republicans should do everything in our power to undo it."

Yet, late in the campaign, after Hagan repeatedly called for North Carolina to expand Medicaid and accept money for healthcare coverage for up to 500,000 residents, Tillis moderated his position on the state expanding its program, and called for repealing Obamacare, but he also spoke about how any reform bill would also need to have provisions for transitioning those people who were already benefiting from the ACA. This more-tempered position may have been guided by polls that showed North Carolina residents to be the least resistant to Medicaid expansion out of four southern states (Arkansas, Kentucky, Louisiana, and North Carolina).[2] Hagan claimed that Tillis showed support for the law in a talk radio interview. Tillis said at one point, "It's a great idea that can't be paid for," and the Hagan camp took the "It's a great idea" portion as an endorsement for Obamacare. PolitiFact checked Hagan's claim and rated it "mostly false" as part of a quote that was taken out of context (L. Jacobson 2014). The incident reflected attempts by both candidates to try to have it both ways on the issue without appearing to be too extreme for the state's electorate.

In the closest of the Senate races studied here, Tillis defeated Hagan by a 1.7 percent margin. Possibly Tillis was less outspoken late in the campaign due to the related debate over Medicaid expansion in the Tar Heel state. Still, in a state that Obama won in 2008 but lost in 2012, the turnout was highest among white voters and not strong in the African American communities and Tillis defeated the one-term Hagan.

## CONCLUSION

The class of senators that rode in on Barack Obama's presidential coattails in 2008 was ushered out of office in 2014. The sixth year of the president's term, his less-than-majority job approval rating, and the unpopularity of his healthcare, immigration, and economic policies drove angry Republicans to the polls and kept many Democrats absent from voting. Republicans gained majority control of the Senate, increased their lead in the House, held key gubernatorial seats and pulled upset wins in three liberal-leaning states (Maryland, Massachusetts, and Illinois). The GOP also picked up more state legislative seats across the country.

The reasons why any one candidate wins or loses are usually numerous in any given campaign. While other issues were important, the ACA may have cost Democrats the electoral majority in Congress it had achieved in 2008. In part, the passage of the law cost the Democrats control of the House with the 2010 Midterm Elections. In 2014 four Democratic incumbents lost their seats in red states (Alaska, Arkansas, Louisiana, and North Carolina). In two open seats (Iowa and Georgia) where they hoped to compete they lost, and in one Republican-incumbent state, Kentucky, where Democrats initially thought they would have a chance, the veteran McConnell won reelection by a 15.5 percent margin of victory.

From evaluation of polls, Obamacare was not the top issue for voters. While the discussions over repealing Obamacare and the costs of healthcare plans were common talking points for rousing the Republican Party base, they were not a primary vehicle for motivating voters to make their decisions. While a majority of people in the states examined said the ACA went too far, just fewer than 50 percent felt that it was about right or did not go far enough. The advantage was to Republicans on the issue of Obamacare, but it does not appear to be the main reason behind the Republican victory wave in 2014. The ACA combined with relative disapproval of President Obama's job, the sixth-year midterm, and a Senate electoral map favoring Republicans fueled the GOP victories examined here.

NOTES

1. The other one was Gary Peters from Michigan. Peters won his race 55-41 percent while Braley lost.

2. The *New York Times* Upshot/Kaiser Family Foundation Southern States Poll (conducted April 8–15, 2014), http://s3.documentcloud.org/documents/1146701/polls-in-four-southern-states-april-8-15-2014.pdf.

Chapter 10

# Immigration Reform and the 2014 Midterms
## The Politics of Executive Action
*Heather Silber Mohamed*

While President Obama's name was not on the ballot in the 2014 Midterm Elections, the contest was frequently characterized as a mandate on his policies. Ironically, however, a significant amount of preelection debate focused on a policy the president did *not* enact: an executive order on comprehensive immigration reform. In the wake of an ongoing congressional stalemate over this issue, President Obama declared in June 2014 that he would undertake executive action to provide relief to some of the estimated eleven million immigrants living in the United States without legal status (Davis and Preston 2014). Three months later, Obama changed course, announcing that he would postpone any executive action until after the election. In this chapter, I examine the competing politics around this issue, including the president's decision to propose, and then postpone, unilateral action. With the 2016 presidential elections placing immigration back into the political spotlight, an understanding of the intraparty tensions surrounding this issue, as well as the varied ways that the immigration debate continues to influence electoral politics and policymaking in the United States, is particularly timely.

In recent years, press coverage about the inability to enact comprehensive immigration reform has typically focused on the split between moderate and conservative Republicans (see, for instance, Ferraro and Yonglai 2013; and Caldwell 2014). Far less attention is paid to the conflicting political pressures that confront Democrats. After President Obama's June 2014 announcement, intraparty tensions surfaced, as moderate Democratic senators in close reelection contests spoke out against his plans to act unilaterally. Here, I explore a number of questions: Why did Obama first consider executive action? Why did some Democratic senators urge the president to wait until after the election? How was the immigration debate poised to influence these contests? And, how did different constituencies—particularly Latino voters—respond to these events? To answer these questions, I draw on recent scholarship as well as press coverage and public opinion data.

## POLITICAL DEMOGRAPHY AND THE DEBATE OVER IMMIGRATION REFORM

Recent elections in the United States have been characterized by an increasingly diverse electorate. Over the last two decades, the vote share of whites has declined from 84.6 percent in 1992 to 72 percent in 2008, while that of minorities has steadily increased (Taylor 2012). As the president weighed whether or not to undertake executive action, he faced a balancing act of politics and demography: appealing to Latino voters, the majority of which seek sweeping changes to immigration policy, while also retaining support from white voters, many of whom oppose such reforms.

In recent years, the Latino vote share has grown rapidly, increasing from 3.8 percent in 1992 to an estimated 10 percent in 2012. Latinos were also a key segment of the "Obama coalition" of young, minority, and women voters that helped elect the president in 2008 and reelect him in 2012 (Lopez et al. 2014). Substantial variation exists in Latino attitudes toward immigration policy (Knoll 2012; Silber Mohamed 2017; Rouse, Wilkinson, and Garand 2010), and immigration issues are certainly not the only policy issue to influence this community's electoral choices. In fact, when asked about the most important public policy issue, Latinos have long prioritized social policies such as education, the economy/jobs, and healthcare over immigration (Lopez, Gonzalez-Barrera, and Krogstad 2014; Rouse, Wilkinson, and Garand 2010). Paradoxically, however, the immigration debate appears poised to mobilize certain Latino voters unlike any other issue (Silber Mohamed 2017), with a majority indicating that immigration policy influenced either their enthusiasm for an election or their vote choice (Latino Decisions 2014).

With respect to white voters, a long trajectory of scholarship underscores the role of race and symbolic politics in shaping political attitudes and preferences, focusing in particular on responses to an African American outgroup (Carmines and Stimson 1989; Kinder and Sanders 1996; Kinder and Kam 2012; Tesler and Sears 2010). Increasing evidence demonstrates that attitudes toward immigrants likewise influence the partisan affiliation of whites (Hajnal and Rivera 2014; Abrajano and Hajnal 2015). Indeed, while minority support for Democrats has grown in recent years, white support has significantly decreased, with immigration policy accounting for some of this shift (Abrajano and Hajnal 2015). The centrality of immigration to the 2016 presidential contest further exemplifies this trend: Republican nominee Donald J. Trump made the construction of a wall on the US–Mexico border a focal point of his campaign, evoking enthusiastic chants of "Build the Wall" by supporters at his events (Parker, Corasaniti, and Berenstein 2016; Tesler 2016).

Among some white voters, the immigration policy debate has become a "wedge issue," with the power to push even those who are not initially anti-immigration toward the Republican Party (Neiman, Johnson, and Bowler 2006; Hajnal and Rivera 2014). Underscoring this shift is a burgeoning narrative in which immigrants represent a threat to jobs, national security, and traditional American culture (Chavez 2008; Huntington 2004a, 2004b; Hainmueller and Hopkins 2014; Branton et al. 2011). Given that Democrats are thought to support immigrants and Republicans are seen as opposing almost all action on immigration, many white Americans might perceive these associations as "a powerful motivation to defect to the Republican Party" (Hajnal and Rivera 2014, 776).

While the movement of white voters away from the Democratic Party began well before the current immigration debate, in recent years it has been reinforced by this conflict. For instance, according to data from the American National Election Study, while 39 percent of whites identified as Democrats in 1980, by 2010 that figure declined to 29 percent; during the same period Republicans saw a corresponding increase among white identifiers, from 28 percent to 36 percent (Abrajano and Hajnal 2015).

## POLICY CONTEXT: FAILED IMMIGRATION DEBATES AND THE GROWING CALL FOR EXECUTIVE ACTION

Until the 1990s, the immigration issue defied clear partisan lines. Indeed, previous iterations of immigration reform received broad support, and legislation was frequently characterized by "strange bedfellows" uniting for action (Tichenor 2002, 2014). In recent years, however, the debate has become increasingly partisan. To some extent, this shift dates back to California's 1994 referendum on Proposition 187, which sought to deny immigrants access to a range of social services. The partisan rhetoric surrounding this debate eventually shifted to the national level (Miller and Schofield 2008; Wong et al. 2013; Ayón 2006; Silber Mohamed 2017), where efforts to enact comprehensive immigration reform have been stymied for over a decade (Tichenor 2014).

Proposals for comprehensive reform encompass a range of issues, including border security and immigration enforcement. By far the most contentious topic has been the question of what to do with the estimated 11–12 million immigrants currently in the United States without legal status, and whether or not these individuals should be given a path to US citizenship (Leal 2014). Since the early 2000s, the Senate has passed several bipartisan bills including provisions for such a path, but conservative Republicans, particularly in the House of Representatives, have repeatedly blocked these proposals, charging that citizenship would constitute "amnesty" for undocumented immigrants.

Following failed attempts at comprehensive immigration reform in both 2006 and 2007, then-presidential candidate Obama pledged to enact immigration reform during his first year in office. Among Latino voters, this pledge became known as *La Promesa de Obama* (Obama's promise). Once elected, however, the financial crisis and healthcare reform quickly superseded immigration policy. Not only did Obama fail to pass comprehensive immigration reform, but Congress also remained deadlocked even on less controversial proposals like the DREAM Act, which would have provided a path to citizenship for certain individuals brought to the United States by their parents at a very young age. Moreover, during his first term, President Obama enacted several policies that many Latinos thought to be harsh. For instance, deportations of undocumented immigrants grew to unprecedented levels—1.4 million by July 2012, a substantial rise over previous administrations (Khimm 2012). The president also enacted several other policies related to immigration enforcement that angered many in the Latino community, such as increased collaboration between local and federal officials on immigration enforcement (for details, see Wallace 2012).

Prior to the 2012 General Election, Latinos increasingly vocalized their critique of the president for breaking *La Promesa de Obama* to enact immigration reform in his first year. Likewise, personalities in the Spanish-language media drew significant attention to this issue. In particular, Jorge Ramos, a renowned news anchor for Spanish-language network Univision, repeatedly warned that the president had a "credibility problem" among Latinos for this broken promise (Brown 2010). In a 2012 preelection interview conducted in Spanish using simultaneous translation, Ramos emphasized this frustration, switching to English and imploring the president, "Before I continue, I want for you to acknowledge that you did not keep your promise" (The White House 2012). Latino disappointment with the president was also evident in public opinion surveys. For instance, according to Gallup polls from early 2010, Latino support for Obama decreased from 69 percent in January to 57 percent in May, while no similar shifts were evident among whites or African Americans (Brown 2010).

In the wake of this frustration, in June 2012 the president announced a new program, Deferred Action for Childhood Arrivals (DACA), to provide temporary employment status—though not a path to citizenship—for young people who would have been covered under the Development, Relief, and Education for Alien Minors (DREAM) Act. With the presidential election just months away, critics argued that this program was an overtly political move to appeal to Latino voters (Dade and Halloran 2012). Indeed, polls demonstrated DACA's appeal to this electorate: within a week of the program's announcement, an estimated 58 percent of Latinos reported being more enthusiastic about the president (Latino Decisions 2012).

An estimated 71 percent of Latinos supported Obama in 2012, representing a 4 percent increase over 2008 (Lopez et al. 2014). Many attributed the president's strong showing to his new policy of deferred action, as well as broader differences on immigration policy with Republican opponent Mitt Romney.[1] Given the president's strong support from Latino voters, after the election many Republicans suggested that it was finally time to act on immigration reform, so as not to alienate Latino voters in future contests (Leal 2014; Bush and Bolick 2013). Indeed, while Romney received just 23 percent of the Latino vote, Republican President George W. Bush received 40 percent, representing the most decisive drop in support by any racial or ethnic group for one party (Bergman, Segura, and Barreto 2014). This dramatic shift suggests a relative openness to Republican candidates by Latino voters, who demonstrate particularly low levels of partisanship (Hajnal and Lee 2011).

Responding to these political pressures, in the spring and summer of 2013, a bipartisan "Gang of Eight" of Republican and Democratic senators developed a comprehensive reform proposal (S. 744) that passed the Senate by a vote of 68-23.[2] Once again, however, divisions between Republicans in the House and the Senate prevented passage, as Speaker of the House John Boehner (R-OH) refused to bring the bill up for a vote in that chamber.

## EXECUTIVE ACTION AND THE 2014 MIDTERMS

For a number of years, Latino leaders pushed President Obama to undertake executive action in the absence of comprehensive immigration reform legislation. Initially, Obama argued that this approach was beyond his constitutional authority. For instance, in a 2011 televised town hall with Univision, the president proclaimed, "There are enough laws on the books by Congress that are very clear in terms of how we have to enforce our immigration system that for me to simply through executive order ignore those congressional mandates would not conform with my appropriate role as President" (Univision 2011). Obama gradually began to change his position, however, when confronted with continued delays by Congress and growing pressure from the Latino community.

The 2012 DACA program marked the president's first major executive action toward immigration reform. Two years later, Obama announced plans for an expansion of this program. Invoking the partisan nature of the immigration debate, he asserted, "While I will continue to push House Republicans to drop the excuses and act—and I hope their constituents will, too—America cannot wait forever for them to act" (Davis and Preston 2014). Obama declared that he would use executive authority to unilaterally act by the end of the summer.

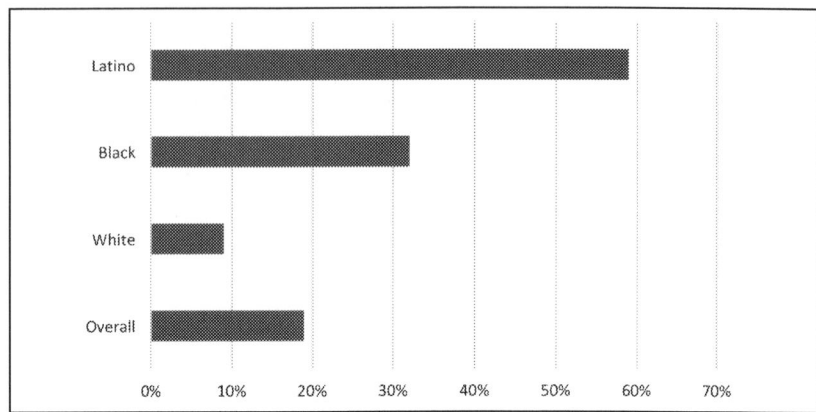

**Figure 10.1.** Difference in Percentage of Respondents Who Very Strongly Approve of Executive Action on Immigration and Those Who Disapprove, by Racial/Ethnic Group

*Source: Pew Research Center, December 2014. Respondents were asked, "As you may know, Barack Obama recently issued an executive action that expands the number of undocumented immigrants who are allowed to stay and work in the country. Overall, do you approve or disapprove of this new policy?" (n=1,454)*

Americans were closely divided in response to the president's proclamation. In a *Washington Post–ABC News* poll (2014) conducted the first week of September 2014, respondents were asked whether the president should undertake executive action on immigration if Congress failed to pass legislation. Among registered voters, 49 percent said that Obama should, while 47 percent said he should not. As figure 10.1 indicates, however, considerable variation was evident when looking across racial and ethnic groups, with 59 percent of Latinos expressing strong support for executive action, compared to just 21 percent of whites.

In the 2014 Midterm Elections, many Democrats faced a balancing act, as incumbents sought to appeal to enough Latino voters to maintain their support without alienating too many white voters.

*Immigration and the Contested Senate Races*

Table 10.1 presents demographic information for six of the Senate seats that were most thought to be "in play," or competitive for either party, in the 2014 midterms. The table also includes information about the relative vote share of the Latino population in each state and the percent change in the state's Latino population between 2000 and 2010. Immigration is thought to be particularly influential as a wedge issue among white voters living amid a fast-growing Latino population (Abrajano and Hajnal 2015; Hopkins 2014). Accordingly, I anticipate that senators in states with the largest Latino population growth (North Carolina and Arkansas) would be most vocal on this issue.

**Table 10.1.** Demographics and Outcome of Select Senate Races, November 2014 Midterm Elections

| Democratic Incumbent (State) | Republican Opponent | Percent Increase in Latino Population, 2000–2010* | Percent Latino Among All Eligible Voters** | Percentage of White Vote Received, Democrat–Republican | Overall Vote Share, Democrat–Republican |
|---|---|---|---|---|---|
| Mark Begich (AK) | Dan Sullivan | 57.9% | 4.8% | 44%–51% | 49%–45% |
| Mark Pryor (AR) | Tom Cotton | 112.9% | 2.9% | 31%–65% | 57%–39% |
| Mark Udall (CO) | Cory Gardner | 42.5 % | 14.2% | 43%–53% | 49%–46% |
| **Mary Landrieu** (LA)*** | Bill Cassidy | 73.5% | 2.8% | 18%–59% | 41%–42% |
| Kay Hagan (NC) | **Thom Tillis** | 113.5% | 3.1% | 33%–62% | 49%–47% |
| **Jeanne Shaheen** (NH) | Scott Brown | 66.6% | 2% | 51%–48% | 52%–48% |

*Sources: Pew Research Center \*(2012) and \*\*(2014); National Exit Poll (2014). Bolded names indicate winner of the November 2014 contest. \*\*\* Vote totals refer to a three-way race between Landrieu and two Republicans in November 2014. Landrieu lost to Cassidy (56-44%) in a runoff election in December 2014.*

After the president announced his policy proposal, some Democratic senators publicly objected to unilateral action. Consistent with the expectations outlined above, in July North Carolina's Senator Hagan was the first to urge the president not to take executive action. As the summer progressed, opposition from moderate Democrats facing reelection grew louder, particularly among those in the South (Kim and Everett 2014). In September Senators Landrieu, Pryor, and Shaheen joined Hagan in her stance against executive action. While these senators had all voted for the Senate's 2013 comprehensive immigration reform proposal, months later they joined a Republican effort to block Obama from enacting unilateral policy change.[3]

Further complicating Obama's decision, in the weeks following his announcement, an estimated 57,000 unaccompanied minors fleeing violence in Central America arrived in the United States (Archibold 2014). Images of tens of thousands of children crossing the border renewed concerns on both sides of the debate. In a sign of growing bitterness, intraparty divisions among Republicans prevented the passage of even an emergency spending proposal to respond to this humanitarian crisis.

*The Delay*

In the lead-up to the election, President Obama faced an undesirable choice: break a second promise to the Latino community and risk losing some of their support, or enact a policy that would threaten the white voter base of moderate and conservative Democrats in tight reelection contests. On September 6 the president announced that he would postpone executive action until after the election. He cited the concern that any action would push politicians in both parties toward even more polarized rhetoric, and might serve to energize anti-immigrant forces on the Republican side (Shear 2014). Obama's decision to postpone executive action was greeted with criticism from across the political spectrum. A sampling of headlines demonstrates this range of critiques: from "Obama's Immigration Train Wreck" in the *Washington Post* (Rubin 2014) to the BBC's "Obama Blasted for Immigration Delay" (Zurcher 2014) to the *Hill*'s "Immigration Activists Rip Obama" (Barron-Lopez 2014). Republicans accused the president of "playing politics" with immigration reform, while Latino leaders complained about a "betrayal" and another broken promise to their community. Presente.org, the largest online Latino activist organization, berated the president and even ran Spanish-language radio ads against Senator Hagan in North Carolina (Shear 2014).

According to the 2014 National Exit Poll, just 14 percent of all voters indicated that immigration was the most important issue facing the country (National Exit Poll 2014). In contrast, a national survey of 4,200 Latino voters conducted between October 20 and November 3, 2014, found nearly half of all respondents listed immigration as the one or two

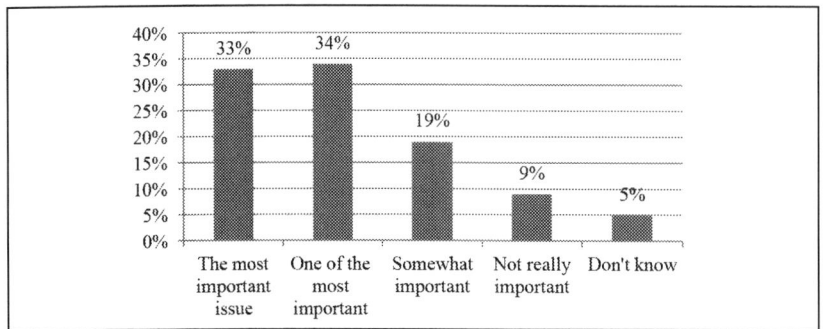

**Figure 10.2.** Latino Attitudes about the Importance of Immigration, 2014

*Source: Latino Decisions Election Eve Poll, November 2014. Respondents were asked, "How important is the issue of immigration in your decision to vote, and who to vote for in this election?" (n=4200)*

most important issues facing their community (Latino Decisions 2014).[4] As figure 10.2 reflects, 67 percent of Latinos reported that immigration was one of the most important issues in determining their vote. Across the sample, an estimated 45 percent stated that immigration reform/the DREAM Act was the top priority issue facing the Latino/Hispanic community; out of ten states studied, Latino voters were most likely to prioritize immigration policy in Georgia and North Carolina (57 percent), both of which have experienced rapid Latino population growth (Latino Decisions 2014).

Among Latinos, the question for many was not whether voters would choose between Republicans and Democrats, but whether to abstain from voting altogether, as pundits and scholars alike questioned whether group members would stay home (Bergman, Segura, and Barreto 2014). In a 2014 survey of two hundred Latinos who were registered to vote but did not plan to cast a ballot, 60 percent reported that the delay made them less enthusiastic about the president and the Democratic Party, suggesting that inaction on immigration might have led some Latino voters to stay home on Election Day (Latino Decisions 2014). Additionally, substantially more voters (48 percent) than nonvoters (33 percent) indicated that they thought Democrats truly cared about Latinos, with 60 percent of the nonvoters indicating that the president's delay made them somewhat less or much less enthusiastic about the Democratic Party. Turnout figures tell a similar story: even as the percentage of eligible Latino voters increased from 8.6 percent to 11.1 percent between 2006 and 2014, Latinos constituted just 8 percent of actual voters in each of these contests, suggesting that an enthusiasm gap may have kept many away from the polls in 2014 (Krogstad and Lopez 2014).

As table 10.1 demonstrates, with the exception of Senator Shaheen, all the moderate Democrats urging the president not to act unilaterally lost their seats in 2014, despite the president's decision to delay. The table also demonstrates the challenges faced by moderate Democrats in the South, with Senators Hagan, Pryor, and Landrieu faring particularly poorly among white voters. Hagan, who was most vocal in her opposition to the president acting unilaterally, received 63 percent of the Latino vote, the lowest level of support for any of the Democratic Senate candidates (Latino Decisions 2014). Despite her public opposition to Obama, Hagan also faced challenges in convincing those who cared most about the immigration debate to support her candidacy. Among respondents who indicated in the National Exit Poll that illegal immigration was the most important policy issue, just 21 percent supported Hagan, while 73 percent supported her opponent, Republican Thom Tillis.

## LESSONS FOR THE FUTURE

In recent years, most discussion of the immigration debate has focused either on Latino attitudes and mobilization, or on divisions within the Republican Party. In this chapter, I demonstrate the strategic challenges faced by Democrats as they attempt to build support among a growing Latino constituency, while also trying to maintain the support of white voters for whom immigration may be a wedge issue. In the short term, Obama's decision to postpone executive action in 2014 appears to have been a losing one: most moderate Democrats who pushed the delay lost their seats, and Latino voters grew increasingly frustrated by repeated broken promises from the president. Not long after the election, Obama proceeded with an executive order anyway, leading many to further question the political calculus behind his delay.

Of course, the president cannot address all immigration issues on his own, and the intraparty challenges faced by both Republicans and Democrats will confront future politicians until Congress acts on immigration reform, and likely beyond. Moreover, as the percentage of white voters gradually shrinks and the ranks of Latino voters grow, the political calculus surrounding this issue will continue to evolve.

## NOTES

1. Specifically, while Obama renewed calls for comprehensive immigration reform, Romney advocated for a policy of "self-deportation," which called for policies that would make undocumented immigrants' lives so difficult that group members would ultimately decide to leave the country on their own.

2. The "Gang of Eight" consisted of four Democratic and four Republican senators, including Senators Michael Bennet (D-CO), Richard Durbin (D-IL), Jeff Flake (R-AZ), Lindsey Graham (R-SC), John McCain (R-AZ), Bob Menendez (D-NJ), Marco Rubio (R-FL), and Chuck Schumer (D-NY).

3. They were also joined by Senator Joe Manchin (D-WV), who was not up for reelection himself, though his state did have an open-seat contest.

4. The poll was sponsored by the Latino Victory Project, the National Council of La Raza, and America's Voice. It was also supported by organizations including People for the American Way, NALEO, AFL-CIO, and Mi Familia Vota.

Chapter 11

# The Climate and Carbon Conservative Campaign Conundrum
## Republicans on Energy and Environment in the 2014 Elections
*Mark J. O'Gorman*

Colorado Republicans were intrigued to see a summer 2014 advertisement of wind turbines whirling in a field of flowers, followed by smiling Republican US Senate candidate Cory Gardner strolling into the frame and saying to the camera, "So, what's a Republican, like me, doing at a wind farm?" (Gardner, "Next Generation Energy" 2014). He answered, stating:

> Supporting the next generation, that's what. I'm Cory Gardner. I cowrote the law to launch our state's clean energy industry. Now I'm working across party lines to encourage the natural gas our economy needs. Growth. And opportunity. From the Earth. For Colorado. That's what's right for our future. That's why I approve this message. Announcer: Gory Gardner. A new generation. A new kind of Republican.

Political observers criticized overstatements in Gardner's ad, clarifying that the clean energy agency law he cowrote failed and was abandoned, while progressives and ecological groups railed against Republican Gardner's attempt to claim environmental issues for his own (Blake 2014; Wyatt 2014). Of greater value, Gardner's ad hints at a complex set of tactics that GOP candidates used in the 2014 Midterm Elections to respond to climate change and energy issues. Tactics, while successful in helping the GOP retake the US Senate, are all-but-moot in a Republican Party led by Donald Trump.

Conflicting environmental and energy issues, traditionally less important to voters in US political campaigns, are quickly gaining import in the American political landscape. In the same summer as Gardner's ad, the US National Climate Assessment released a global climate change (GCC) impact report, detailing the many impacts "already affecting the American people…disrupting people's lives and damaging some sectors of our economy" (US Global Change Research Program 2014). Despite such warnings, fossil-fuel energy production, driven by natural gas extraction and hydraulic fracturing (fracking) technologies, turned the United States into the world's leading energy producer in 2012, and the world's top producer of crude oil in 2014 (Blackwill and O'Sullivan 2014). Jobs and economic growth surges in multiple American states due to fracking development created opportunities for 2014 GOP incumbents and candidates to trumpet successful fossil-fuel-fueled entrepreneurship, while criticizing government regulations that inhibit market-based growth. Whether pro-energy or antienvironmental regulation focused, oil, gas, and energy themed campaign advertisements were among the most prominent in the 2014 midterms (Rogers 2014; O'Connor 2014).

GOP political professionals recognized in 2014, however, that ignoring growing GCC concerns courts electoral danger. No longer just a progressive issue easily dismissed as left-wing rants against the oil and gas industry, climate change concerns have clear traction among US voters. A *New York Times*, Stanford University, and Resources for the Future (RFF) January 2015 poll showed 81 percent of people surveyed saying climate change was caused at least in part by human activities, with 88 percent of Democrats, 84 percent of Independents and 71 percent of Republicans saying climate change was caused by humans.

If this trend continues, strident conservative antienvironmental rhetoric could create problems for the GOP in future US elections. Can the

Republican Party create a platform that is both pro–carbon extraction, and also pro–climate change? How do mainstream Republicans work with evangelical Christian and Tea Party factions to develop centrist energy and environmental policies in national elections? Can Republicans attract new voters, given that growing demographic groups do not share GOP views on climate change and the future role of carbon in America? Analyzing GOP state and national party platforms, GOP Senate candidate public statements, debate answers and campaign ads, reveals delicate campaign approaches to carbon energy and climate change, mixing traditional climate-denial posturing with other tactics, suggesting a conscious strategy in 2014 that, if repeated, endangers 2018 and 2020 GOP candidates.

## THE REPUBLICAN'S 2014 CARBON/CLIMATE CAMPAIGN STRATEGY

How did the Republican Party address carbon and climate issues in 2014? Strategically, "the political texture" of specific state/districts races, along with national factors, favored Republicans (Abramowitz 2014; G. C. Jacobson 2013). Democrats defended twenty-one Senate seats, compared with fifteen for Republicans (Kapur 2014). Many Senate Democratic seats were in traditionally conservative "red" states, including seven state races that GOP presidential candidate Mitt Romney carried in 2012 (Cook 2014). Older, Caucasian, and wealthier midterm voter-turnout demographics plus strong GOP voter opposition to President Obama also favored Republicans (Wasserman 2013).

Republicans saw advantages in their party's staunch defense of fossil fuels. Their party's energy platform for 2014 rested on making "America energy independent by encouraging investment in domestic energy, lowering prices, and creating jobs at home" ("Midterm Election Strategy" 2014). Building on the GOP 2012 national party platform calling for an all-of-the-above US energy policy, due to being "blessed with abundant energy resources, tapped and untapped, traditional and alternative," that prioritized coal, oil, and natural gas, and nuclear energy development before renewable energy sources (We Believe in America 2012), GOP state 2014 party platforms reinforced fossil fuel–centered support, whether endorsing oil and gas subsidies or removal of drilling fees by Texas

Republicans, or championing coal extraction by Indiana Republicans (Texas Republican Party 2014; Indiana Republican Party 2014).

Shale gas production, utilizing horizontal drilling and hydraulic fracturing (aka fracking) technologies has creating the greatest increase in US fossil fuel energy production in many decades. From 2007 to 2012, "US shale gas production rose over 50 percent annually, and its share of total US gas production jumped from 5 percent to 39 percent" (Blackwill and O'Sullivan 2014, 102–4). Between 2007 and 2012, an eighteenfold increase in US production of high quality "light tight oil" occurred, leading to a 50 percent increase in US crude oil production. In 2013 the United States passed Russia as the world's leading energy producer, and in 2015 International Energy Agency (IEA) projections showed that the United States will overtake Saudi Arabia as the top producer of crude oil (Blackwill and O'Sullivan 2014). In April 2014 the United States produced 8.4 million barrels of oil per day, a production total not seen since 1988 (Institute for Energy Research 2014). In June 2014 IEA confirmed that the United States was the world's "biggest producer of oil and natural gas liquids" (Smith 2014).

Coal, natural gas, and oil development were a critical component of the state level focus in many competitive Senate races. In states where Republicans won seats previously held by Democrats (Alaska, Arkansas, Colorado, Iowa, Louisiana, Montana, North Carolina, South Dakota, and West Virginia), three states (Colorado, Montana, and West Virginia) were in the top ten for coal reserves with three other states in the top half of states with coal reserves (Iowa, Louisiana, and South Dakota) (Richardson et al. 2013). Alaska, Colorado, and Louisiana were in the top ten for proven oil reserves (Sauter 2013). Six of the states (Alaska, Arkansas, Colorado, Louisiana, Montana, and West Virginia) were among the top ten states with the largest 2007–2012 oil and gas employment change (US Bureau of Labor Statistics 2014).

Mitch McConnell, Republican Senate minority leader in 2014, released a July 2014 television ad entitled "Different Direction," attacking his opponent's fossil energy record. As the screen was filled with the statement, "Alison Lundergan Grimes supports Barack Obama's anticoal environmental platform, McConnell is heard saying: 'We want to go in a different direction. We want to have an America that celebrates success, gets jobs for people who are hurting, and that stops the War on Coal now'" (Youngman 2014).

Despite GOP carbon economy advantages in 2014, climate concerns among Independent and Republican voters suggested to GOP candidates that exclusive climate-denial attack tactics could create blowback, especially in close races. With over 60 percent of those polled in 2014 polls by Gallup, Stanford University, and Yale University agreeing that climate change is happening, GOP state 2014 platforms revealed a delicate merge of pro oil/gas and GCC-focused policy positions ("Polling the American Public" 2014). Alaska's 2014 state GOP platform supported "alternative, sustainable energy sources such as geothermal, hydro, solar, tidal, and wind," but only when economically viable, a free-market focus trending among other 2014 state GOP platforms in Indiana and Texas (Alaska Republican Party 2014).

During the 2014 US Senate campaign, a review of GOP Senate campaign debate responses reveals four climate change issue response tactics: denial of climate change; blaming Obama for fomenting a climate frenzy; recusing themselves from the issue given their lack of climate science expertise; and suspending judgment until later, after more scientific study was done. In sum, they created the GOP's 2014 DORSS (pronounced "doors") climate change/carbon strategy of Denial, Obama's wrong, Recuse, and Suspend Science.

*Denial*

The 2008 GOP party platform on climate change mirrors intraparty shifting climate sands over the past decade. While condemning "doomsday climate change scenarios," and "no-growth radicalism," the platform also called on creating "solutions that will decrease emissions, reduce excess greenhouse gases in the atmosphere [and] mitigate the impact of climate change where it occurs" (Plumer 2012). By 2013 polling showed that while two-thirds of Americans said there is solid global warming evidence, only 46 percent of Republicans agreed (Pew Research 2013b). By 2012, the GOP party platform's climate change section no longer existed and included frequent criticisms of the topic's validity (Plumer 2012).

The rise of the Tea Party faction of the Republican Party amplified such intraparty climate-denial numbers. The 2013 poll showed 61 percent of non–Tea Party Republicans said global warming evidence is real, while only 25 percent of Tea Party respondents agreed (Pew Research 2013b).

With predicted low voter turnout, amplifying passionate ideological extreme voters, GOP candidates had to understand their districts and measure their denials of GCC existence in their elections. Minnesota's 2014 GOP state party platform adopted the denial strategy, opposing "policies, legislation and mandates that are based on the theory that humans are responsible for global climate change including the Theory of Man-Made Global Warming [*sic*]" (Minnesota Republican Party 2014). Texas's GOP 2014 platform put GCC in quotes, implying it was fictional, stating it was "a political agenda which attempts to control every aspect of our lives," urging "government at all levels to ignore any plea for money to fund global climate change" initiatives (Texas Republican Party 2014).

In Colorado, when Cory Gardner was asked in a televised debate if humans significantly contribute to climate change, he stated, "Well, I've said all along climate is changing.... This is an important issue and I don't think you can say yes or no,... I believe climate is changing, but I disagree to the extent that's been in the news that man is changing" (Timm 2014). Shelley Moore Capito, the Republican running for the West Virginia Senate seat stated, "I don't necessarily think the climate's changing, no" (Bobic 2014). Mitch McConnell, Republican Senate minority leader running for reelection in Kentucky said about climate change that, "For everybody who thinks it's warming, I can find somebody who thinks it isn't" (Wartman 2014a; Atkin 2014).

*Under O'ttack: Blame Obama*

> *I've heard arguments from both sides. I do believe in protecting our environment, but without the job-killing regulations that are coming out of the [Environmental Protection Agency].... Let's shut down the EPA. The state knows best how to protect resources.*
> *—Joni Ernst, quoted in Adler 2014*

Richard Fenno (1978) once observed that members of Congress run *for* Congress by running *against* Congress. Congressional scholars and political practitioners consistently reveal a decades-long anti–Washington, DC, meme in American politics. Barack Obama gave Republicans a target-rich environment from which to aim their anti-Washington attacks, and to recruit conservative voters. A June 2014 Pew Research polling showed conservatives' support of Obama at less than 5 percent, between mainstream and ideological conservatives (96 percent anti-Obama and 94 percent anti-Obama, respectively) (Pew Research 2014).

Obama exacerbated Republican enmity with his opposition of the Keystone XL (KXL) pipeline. The pipeline, an upgrade of existing pipe infrastructure runs east through Canada from the tar-sands of Western Canada then turns south into the United States, running roughly parallel to US refineries and offloading ports in Louisiana and Texas, and diagonally forming the hypotenuse of the existing pipeline from Alberta to the Gulf of Mexico. KXL supporters spoke of energy security, greater oil transport capacity, and the creation of tens of thousands of pipeline construction jobs (American Petroleum Institute 2015). Although Obama waited until after the 2014 elections to veto KXL-supporting legislation, Obama's public pipeline concerns and April 2014 announcement delaying final decisions until after a Nebraska court challenge was finalized, magnified the use of KXL as an anti-Obama carbon/climate bludgeon (Schor 2014). Obama's diplomatic agreement with Chinese Premier Xi Jingping, committing the United States and China to historic greenhouse gas (GhG) reductions to reduce the impacts of global climate change, only added to the opposition (Sussman 2014).

Tom Cotton, Republican Senate candidate from Arkansas, in response to a US State Department report that the Keystone XL pipeline would not worsen GCC, said:

> Last week, President Obama told us this year would be a 'year of action.' After five years of doing nothing on the Keystone XL pipeline, it's past time that he and Senate Democrats approve a project that will create jobs and move us toward energy independence. (Tom Cotton for Senate 2014).

Congress as an institution consistently polls low, providing Republican challengers more weapons to attack incumbent Democrats, with 2014 no exception. During all of 2014, Pew Research congressional unfavorable levels averaged over 70 percent, with favorable levels averaging just 25 percent, the worst ratings in twenty years of Pew tracking (Pew Research 2015). The rise of the Tea Party wing of the Republican Party in 2009, solidified with the 2010 recapture of majority status in the House of Representatives, confirmed that wing's power, especially in guiding GOP party ideas to the right. Polling of staunchly conservative Tea Party supporters, "the most likely to say they are angry with the federal government," led to GOP US Senate candidate Joni Ernst promising "to abolish" the US Environmental Protection Agency (EPA) in a 2014 television ad (Spross 2014). Texas's 2014 GOP state platform went further: abolish the US EPA, while supporting the "elimination" of the US Department of Energy (Texas Republican Party 2014).

In a September 2014 debate, Alaska Republican Senate candidate Dan Sullivan also preyed upon the antigovernment sentiment of 2014 saying "the jury's out" about climate change, then attacking the 44th president's administration saying, "we shouldn't lock up America's resources and kill tens of thousands of good jobs by continuing to pursue the President's anti-energy policies" (McDonnell 2014). In a North Carolina GOP Senate primary debate, Thom Tillis laughed, along with the other three Republican primary challengers, when asked if they believed climate change is a fact, with Tillis adding to his criticism, saying, "the liberal agenda, the Obama agenda…is trying to use [GCC] as a Trojan horse for their energy policy" (McDonnell 2014).

### Recuse: Claim to Be Unqualified to Answer

Antiscience skepticism polls higher among GOP voters, with less than half of Republicans saying humans have evolved over time, and that number halved again for evolutionary support among White evangelical Protestants (Pew Research Center 2013a). Two-thirds of Democrats, 43 percent of Independents, and just 24 percent of Republicans say global warming is happening mostly because of human activity, while 48 percent said scientists generally do not agree that human activity causes global warming, over twice the number for Democrats and eleven points more than Independent respondents (Pew Research 2013b). While well over 90 percent of climate scientists agree that human activity is accelerating planetary warming and creating greater and more destructive climate-change effects, the lack of absolute unanimity provides conservatives an entry point to challenge the research.

On the campaign trail, this became an opportunity to claim scientific illiteracy. Mitch McConnell, when asked if human activity drove climate change, said, "I'm not a scientist" (Wartman 2014b). McConnell matched comments by other Republican politicians claiming ignorance, including US House Speaker John Boehner, Florida Governor Rick Scott, Louisiana Governor Bobby Jindal, and Florida Senator and 2016 GOP Presidential Candidate Marco Rubio (Atkin 2014).

Joni Ernst also attempted to recuse herself, saying, "I don't know the science behind climate change. I can't say one way or another what is the direct impact, whether it's man-made or not" (Spross 2014). Bill Cassidy, GOP 2014 Senate candidate in Louisiana, added to his doubt a refocus on other important natural resource issues, "I am not sure climate change is the issue as much as getting the sediment out of the Mississippi River is" (O'Donoghue 2014).

*Suspend Science: Need More Time/More Study OR State 'Real' Science Facts*
Minnesota's GOP party platform embrace of "sound science" telegraphs selective rejection of climate-scientist GCC data that does not champion a Christian-centered human stewardship of the planet (Minnesota Republican Party 2014). Texas, Alaska, and Indiana GOP state platforms also used "steward" or "stewardship" phrasing in discussing 2014 environmental policy. Some Senate candidates even attempted to insert their own data, or interpretation of their selected data points, to amplify how uncertain climate change science really was. Cassidy, in an October 2014 debate with Democratic incumbent Senator Mary Landrieu said, "global temperatures have not risen in 15 years" (Colman 2014). Cassidy was incorrect. Ten of the warmest years for global temperatures on record were all since 2000, according to NASA, NOAA, and the World Meteorological Association (Mooney 2015). Data suggests a slowing of the rate of temperature increases during Cassidy's time period, but no global temperature reductions (Colman 2014; Mooney 2015). Frequently, conservative climate critics hold up cold weather in winter as an example showing that the planet is not warming, missing the difference between short-term weather patterns and decades-long climate change that has occurred over much of the last hundred years or so (Leber 2015). Tom Cotton criticized science in numerous ways in his response:

> The simple fact is that for the last 16 years, the Earth's temperature has not warmed. That's the facts.... Now, there's no doubt that the tempera-

ture has risen over the past 150,200 years. It's most likely that human activity has contributed to some of that.... Why would we change the way we live our life on a fundamental, civilizational level based on computer models? (Muro, Rothwell, and Saha 2011).

Every GOP Senate candidate previously analyzed won US Senate seats in 2014. Did their climate change commentary provide the margin of victory? Probably not. But by crafting language in ways that party faithful could support, while minimizing opposition attack, and deflecting attention away from national trends favoring Republican electoral success, the GOP's DORSS tactics worked. Can they work again?

*Climate Change, the US Senate, and the Trump Presidency*

Republicans have command of all branches of the US federal government. Yet, with such an advantage, climate change will influence Republican Senate races in 2018 and beyond. On climate change, the *NYT/RFF/* Stanford poll data showed that twice as many Hispanic respondents rated global warming as more important to them than white respondents, and are much more likely to support government policies to reduce greenhouse gas (GhG) pollution (Davenport and Connelly 2015). 'Sunny-day flooding' in coastal cities like Miami, FL, due to higher seas tide due to climate change, plus larger Hispanic voter turnout in the foreseeable future suggest that the GOP runs risks by maintaining all-carbon and climate-denying campaign strategies.

Climate change polling consistently disadvantages GCC-denying GOP politicians. Yale's 2016 major GCC report showed across-the-board increases in GCC concern, with "conservative Republicans hav[ing] experienced the largest shift of any group—an increase of 19 percentage points over the past two years" (Leiserowitz et al. 2016). While Yale revealed that climate change struggles to be among the top ten voting preferences issues, registered voters are three times as likely to say they would be more likely rather than less likely to vote for a candidate supporting climate change policies, with 43 percent more likely, versus only 14 percent less likely (Leiserowitz, et al. 2016).

A January 2014 Pew poll showed support by both parties for renewable energy, including 58 percent of Republicans (Gilbert 2014). Renewable energy economic development data suggests that Republicans cannot ignore such green market forces. A 2011 Brookings Institution report *Sizing the Clean Economy* showed 2.7 million green industry and/ or renewable energy jobs being created, with consistent double-digit renewable industry growth in a number of states in recent years (Muro, Rothwell, and Saha 2011). National security linkages with climate change, amplifying conflicts within and among nations in Africa and the Middle East, are better documented and show a geopolitical need for the United States to take global action on climate change (O'Gorman 2014).

A sober reality is that the Earth continues to warm. July 2016 was the hottest July on record, and the hottest month ever recorded on the planet (Thompson 2015). It was the fifteenth consecutive month that the global temperature record was broken, a trend never seen in the 137 years of such record keeping (Yulsman 2016). As US Senator Bernie Sanders's (I-VT) passionate primary campaign appeal to fight the scourge of climate change fades into memory, one wonders how the GOP, or even the Democrats, will take on energy and climate issues after a 2016 campaign season of mindboggling fluidity. GOP presidential candidate Donald Trump frequently called climate change a hoax (L. Jacobson 2016). Democrat presidential candidate Hillary Clinton supported climate change policy, but large corporate oil and gas contributions to the Clinton Foundation raised questions as to her climate sincerity (Adler 2015). One hopes that with Donald Trump as 45th US President, he will embrace energy and climate policies that help, not imperil, the planet. Or that the nation will, finally, elect those who will.

# Bibliography

Abrajano, Marisa A., and Zoltan L. Hajnal. 2015. *White Backlash: Immigration, Race, and American Politics*. Princeton, NJ: Princeton University Press.

Abramowitz, Alan I. 2014. "Nationalization of Senate Elections Poses Challenges to Democrats in 2014." Sabato's Crystal Ball, May 22. Accessed May 2, 2015. http://www.centerforpolitics.org/crystalball/articles/nationalization-of-senate-elections-poses-challenge-to-democrats-in-2014/.

Adler, Ben. 2014. "Meet Your New Fossil Fuel-Loving GOP Senators." *Grist*, November 6. Accessed May 4, 2015. http://grist.org/politics/meet-your-new-fossil-fuel-loving-gop-senators/.

Aistrup, Joseph. A. 1996. *The Southern Strategy Revisited: Republican Top-Down Advancement in the South*. Lexington: University Press of Kentucky.

Alaska Republican Party. 2014. "Platform." May 3. Accessed August 27, 2016. http://www.alaskagop.org/platform.

Alesina, Albert, and Howard Rosenthal. *Partisan Politics, Divided Government, and the Economy*. New York: Cambridge University Press, 1995.

Allen, Theodore, and Mikhail Bernshteyn. 2006. "Mitigating Voter Waiting Times." *Chance* 19 (4): 25–34.

Alvarez, Michael R., Stephen Ansolabehere, Adam Berinksy, Gabriel Lenz, Charles Stewart, III, and Thad Hall. 2009. "2008 Survey of the Performance of American Elections Report." California Institute of Technology. http://elections.delaware.gov/pdfs/SPAE_2008.pdf.

American Petroleum Institute. 2015. "Keystone XL Pipeline." Accessed May 4, 2015. http://www.api.org/policy-and-issues/policy-items/keystone-xl/keystone-xl-pipeline.

Arbour, Brian. 2014. "'All Politics is Local'? Not Anymore." *The Monkey Cage*, December 9. Accessed June 15, 2017. https://www.washingtonpost.com/blogs/monkey-cage/wp/2014/12/09/all-politics-is-local-not-anymore/.

Archibold, Randal C. 2014. "Trying to Slow the Illegal Flow of Young Migrants." *New York Times,* July 20. Accessed July 21, 2014. http://www.nytimes.com/2014/07/21/world/americas/trying-to-slow-the-illegal-flow-of-young-migrants-at-the-border-reports-show-decline-in-texas.html?.

Atkin, Emily. 2014. "'I'm Not a Scientist': A Complete Guide to Politicians Who Plead Ignorance on Climate Change." *ThinkProgress,* October 3. Accessed May 7, 2015. http://thinkprogress.org/climate/2014/10/03/3575849/not-a-scientist/.

Ayón, David R. 2006. "Immigration and the 2006 Elections." Woodrow Wilson International Center for Scholars *U.S.-Mexico Policy Bulletin* issue 8 (December): 1–6.

Azari, Julia. 2014. "How National Are the 2014 Elections?" *The New West*, official blog of the Western Political Science Association, November 3. https://thewpsa.wordpress.com/2014/11/03/how-national-are-the-2014-elections/.

Bafumi, Joseph, Robert S. Erikson, and Christopher Wlezien. 2010. "Balancing, Generic Polls, and Midterm Congressional Elections." *Journal of Politics* 72 (3): 705–19.

Ball, Molly. 2014. "Is This the End of the GOP Civil War?" *Atlantic*, May 6. Accessed March 14, 2015. http://www.theatlantic.com/politics/archive/2014/05/thom-tillis-wins-north-carolina-primary-is-this-the-end-gop-civil-war/361834/.

Ballhaus, Rebecca. 2014. "Scott Brown Tries to Put Sullivan County on the Map." *Wall Street Journal*, October 30, 2014.

Barone, Michael, and Richard Cohen. 2004. *Almanac of American Politics.* Washington, DC: National Journal Group.

Barron-Lopez, Laura. 2014. "Immigration Activists Rip Obama." *The Hill*, September 6. Accessed May 1, 2015. http://thehill.com/blogs/blog-briefing-room/news/216855-latino-community-outraged-by-Obamas-immigration-delay.

Bart, John, and James Meader. 2004. "The More You Spend, the Less They Listen: The South Dakota U.S. Senate Race." In *The Last Hurrah?: The Soft Money and Issue Advocacy in the 2002 Congressional Elections*, edited by David B. Magleby and J. Quin Monson, 159–80. Washington, DC: Brookings Institution Press.

Bash, Dana. 2013. "Senate Dem Leaders Holding Off on Legislative 'Fix' for Insurance Promise." *CNN Political Ticker*, November 14.

Bennett, W. Lance. 2003. *News: The Politics of Illusion.* 5th ed. New York: Longman.

Berelson, Bernard. 1952. *Content Analysis in Communication Research.* Glencoe, IL: Free Press.

Bergerson, Peter, and Margaret Banyon. 2015. "Florida's Bellwether Congressional District 13 Race: The Death of Local Politics." In *The Roads to Congress 2014*, edited by Sean D. Foreman and Robert Dewhirst, 125–39. Lanham, MD: Lexington Books.

Bergman, Elizabeth, Gary Segura, and Matt Barreto. 2014. "Immigration Politics and Electoral Consequences: Anticipating the Dynamics of Latino Vote in the 2014 Election." *California Journal of Politics and Policy* 6 (3): 339–59.

Blackwill, Robert D., and Meghan L. O'Sullivan. 2014. "America's Energy Edge." *Foreign Affairs* 93 (2): 102–14. Accessed May 2, 2015. https://www.foreignaffairs.com/articles/united-states/2014-02-12/americas-energy-edge.

Blake, Peter. 2014. "Candidates Swap Scripts in 'Silly Season' of Political Ads." *Complete Colorado*, September 10. Accessed April 19, 2015. http://completecolorado.com/pagetwo/2014/09/10/blake-candidates-swap-scripts-in-silly-season-of-political-ads/.

Bobic, Igor. 2014. "Shelley Moore Capito Says Climate Is Changing Because It's 'Raining' Outside." *Huffington Post*, October 8. Accessed May 7, 2015. http://www.huffingtonpost.com/2014/10/08/capito-climate-change_n_5953796.html.

Bolton, Alexander. 2014. "ObamaCare Author: Health Law Is 'Really Complicated.'" *The Hill*, December 3. Accessed March 14, 2015. http://thehill.com/homenews/senate/225812-harkin-dems-better-off-without-obamacare.

Boonstra, Heather D., and Elizabeth Nash. 2014. "A Surge of State Abortion Restrictions Puts Providers—and the Women They Serve—in the Crosshairs." *Guttmacher Policy Review* 1 (17): 9–15.

Branton, Regina P., Erin S. Cassese, Bradford S. Jones, and Chad Westerland. 2011. "All Along the Watchtower: Acculturation, Fear, Anti-Latino Affect, and Immigration." *Journal of Politics* 73 (3): 664–79.

Brookings Institution. 2014. "Vital Statistics on Congress." Accessed March 5, 2015. https://www.brookings.edu/multi-chapter-report/vital-statistics-on-congress/.

Brown, Carrie Budoff. 2010. "Hispanic Media Take on Obama." *Politico*, August 11. Accessed April 1, 2014. http://www.politico.com/news/stories/0810/40927.html.

Bryer, Thomas, Terri Susan Fine, Michelle Gardner, and Adrienne Mathews. 2011. "Training in Virtual Worlds: Engaging the Next Generation of Poll Workers." *National Social Sciences Technology Journal* 1 (3). Accessed 6.6.2017. http://www.nssa.us/tech_journal/volume_1-3/vol1-3_article_3.htm.

Buell, Duncan A. 2013. "An Analysis of Long Lines in Richland County, South Carolina." *USENIX Journal of Election Technology and Systems* 1:106–18.

Bump, Philip. 2014. "40 Painful Seconds of Alison Lundergan Grimes Refusing to Say Whether She Voted for President Obama." *Washington Post*, October 9. Accessed March 14, 2015. http://www.washingtonpost.com/blogs/the-fix/wp/2014/10/09/40-painful-seconds-of-alison-lundergan-grimes-refusing-to-say-whether-she-voted-for-president-obama/.

Burden, Barry C. and Charles Stewart III (eds.). 2014. *The Measure of American Elections*. New York: Cambridge University Press.

Bush, Jeb, and Clint Bolick. 2013. "A Republican Case for Immigration Reform." *Wall Street Journal*, June 30. Accessed April 1, 2014. http://online.wsj.com/news/articles/.

Caldwell, Leigh Ann. 2014. "A Tale of Two Republicans: A Story of the GOP and Immigration Reform." *CNN Politics*, February 4. Accessed April 30, 2014. http://www.cnn.com/2014/02/04/politics/republican-immigration/index.html.

Campbell, Angus. 1966. "Surge and Decline: A Study of Electoral Change." In *Elections and the Political Order*, edited by Angus E. Campbell, Philip E. Converse, Warren E. Miller, and Donald E. Stokes. New York: Wiley, 40–62.

Campbell, James E., and Joe A. Sumners. 1990. "Presidential Coattails in Senate Elections." *American Political Science Review* 84 (2): 513–24.

Carmines, Edward G., and James A. Stimson. 1989. *Issue Evolution: Race and the Transformation of American Politics*. Princeton, NJ: Princeton University Press.

Carsey, Thomas M., and Gerald C. Wright. 1998. "State and National Factors in Gubernatorial and Senatorial Elections." *American Journal of Political Science* 42 (3): 994–1002.

Chavez, Leo R. 2008. *The Latino Threat: Constructing Immigrants, Citizens, and the Nation*. Stanford, CA: Stanford University Press.

Claassen, Ryan L., David B. Magleby, J. Quin Monson, and Kelly D. Patterson. 2008. "At Your Service: Voter Evaluation of Poll Worker Performance." *American Politics Research* 36 (4): 369–90.

Claggett, William, William Flanigan, and Nancy Zingele. 1984. "Nationalization of the American Electorate." *American Political Science Review* 78 (1): 77–91.

Clozel, Lalita. 2014. "Cash for Challengers: Some Turn the Tables, Outraising Incumbents." *Open Secrets Blog*, November 24. Accessed March 15, 2015. http://www.opensecrets.org/news/2014/11/cash-for-challengers-some-turn-the-tables-outraising-incumbents/.

Cohn, Nate. 2014. "When Even a Good Midterm Turnout for Democrats in North Carolina Fell Short." *New York Times*, December 15. Accessed May 1, 2015. http://www.nytimes.com/2014/12/16/upshot/why-even-a-good-midterm-turnout-for-democrats-in-north-carolina-fell-short.html?.

Colman, Zack. 2014. "Sen. Mary Landrieu, Rep. Bill Cassidy Offer Opposing Climate Change Views." *Washington Examiner*, October 14. Accessed May 7, 2015. http://www.washingtonexaminer.com/sen.-mary-landrieu-rep.-bill-cassidy-offer-opposing-climate-change-views/article/25548098.

Cook, Charlie. 2015. "The GOP's Damage Done: How the Homeland Security Stalemate Is Hurting the Republican Brand." *National Journal*, March 2. Accessed March 14, 2015. http://www.nationaljournal.com/off-to-the-races/the-gos-s-damage-done-20150302.

Cook, Fay Lomax, Tom R. Tyler, Edward G. Goetz, Margaret T. Gordon, David Protess, Donna R. Leff, and Harvey L. Molotch. 1983. "Media and Agenda Setting: Effects of the Public, Interest Group Leaders, Policy Makers, and Policy." *Public Opinion Quarterly* 47 (1): 16–35.

Cook Political Report. 2014. "2014 Senate Race Ratings." November 3. Accessed March 14, 2015. http://cookpolitical.com/senate/charts/race-ratings/8058.

Cook, Rhodes. 2014. "Political Terrain for the 2014 Senate and Gubernatorial Races." *CQ Voting and Elections Collection*, April. Accessed May 2, 2015. http://library.cqpress.com/.

Cooper, Christopher A. 2002. "Media Tactics in the State Legislature." *State Politics & Policy Quarterly* 2 (4): 353–71.

*Concord Monitor*. 2014. Editorial. June 4.

———. 2014b. "A Bluer Shade of Purple, Nothing More." November 6.

———. 2014c. Editorial. October 28.

Cox, Gary W., and Jonathan N. Katz. 1996. "Why Did the Incumbency Advantage in US House Elections Grow?" *American Journal of Political Science* 40 (2): 478–97.

———. 2002. *Elbridge Gerry's Salamander: The Electoral Consequences of the Reapportionment Revolution*. New York: Cambridge University Press.

Current, Richard N. 1967. *Three Carpetbag Governors*. Baton Rouge: Louisiana State University Press.

Dade, Corey, and Liz Halloran. 2012. "President Obama's Immigration Shift Could Bolster Latino Support in November." *National Public Radio blog*, June 15. Accessed June 13, 2013. http://www.npr.org/blogs/itsallpolitics/2012/06/15 /155126911/president-obamas-immigration-shift-could-bolster-latino-support -in-november.

Darr, Joseph and Matthew Levendusky. 2013. "Relying on the Ground Game: The Placement and Effect of Campaign Field Offices." *American Politics Research* 42 (3): 529–48.

Davenport, Coral, and Marjorie Connelly. 2015. "Most Republicans Say They Back Climate Action, Poll Finds." *New York Times*, January 30. Accessed April 29, 2015. http://www.nytimes.com/2015/01/31/us/politics/most-americans -support-government-action-on-climate-change-poll-finds.html.

Davey, Monica. 2015. "Unions Suffer Latest Defeat in Midwest with Signing of Wisconsin Measure." *New York Times*, March 9. Accessed March 15, 2015. https://www.nytimes.com/2015/03/10/us/gov-scott-walker-of-wisconsin-signs -right-to-work-bill.html?.

Davis, Julie Hirschfield, and Julia Preston. 2014. "Obama Says He'll Order Action to Aid Immigrants." *New York Times*, June 30. Accessed April 30, 2015. http:// www.nytimes.com/2014/07/01/us/obama-to-use-executive-action-to-bolster -border-enforcement.html?.

Deslatte, Melinda. 2013. "Mary Landrieu Stung by Rollout of Health Law: Analysis." *Times-Picayune* (New Orleans, LA), November 10.

Detzner, Ken. 2013. "Recommendations for Increased Accessibility and Efficiency in Florida Elections." Florida Department of State. February 4. http://www.dos .state.fl.us/pdf2-4-2013_Recs_for_Increased_Accessibility_and_Efficiency_in _FL_Elections.pdf.

DiStaso, John. 2014. "Brown's Comment Goes Viral, Shaheen Takes Knocks on Obamacare." Granite Status, *New Hampshire Sunday News*, March 30.

Easley, Jason. 2014. "Things Get Worse for Scott Brown as He Has No Idea What State He Is Running for Senate in." *Politicus USA*, June 13. Accessed March 14, 2015. http://www.politicususa.com/2014/06/13/worse-scott-brown-idea-state -running-senate.html.

Edelman, Murray. 1985. "Political Language and Political Reality." *PS: Political Science & Politics* 18 (1): 10–19.

———. 1988. *Constructing the Political Spectacle*. Chicago: University of Chicago Press.

Edelstein, William A. and Arthur D. Edelstein. 2010. "Queuing and Elections: Long Lines, DREs, and Paper Ballots." *Proceedings of the EVT/WOTE 2010*. https://www.usenix.org/legacy/events/evtwote10/tech/full_papers/Edelstein.pdf?.

Ellis, Jonathan. 2014. "Why It's a Close Race for Senate." *Argus Leader* (Sioux Falls, SD), October 13.

Erikson, Robert S. 1972. "Malapportionment, Gerrymandering and Party Fortunes in Congressional Elections." *American Journal of Political Science* 66 (4): 1234–45.

———. 1988. "The Puzzle of Midterm Loss." *Journal of Politics* 50 (4): 1011–59.

———. 1990. "Economic Conditions and the Congressional Vote: A Review of the Macrolevel Evidence." *American Journal of Political Science* 34 (2): 373–99.

———. 2017. "The Congressional Incumbency Advantage over Sixty Years: Measurement, Trends, and Implications." In *Governing in a Polarized Age*, edited by Alan S. Gerber and Eric Schickler, 65–89. New Haven: Yale University Press.

Erikson, Robert S., Olle Folke, and James M. Snyder, Jr. 2015. "A Gubernatorial Helping Hand?: How Governors Affect Presidential Elections." *Journal of Politics* 77 (2): 491–504.

Everett, Burgess, and Jake Sherman. 2014. "Fla. Loss Exposes Dem ACA Disarray." *Politico*, March 12. Accessed September 7, 2016. http://www.politico.com/story/2014/03/obamacare-affordable-care-act-david-jolly-alex-sink-florida-elections-2014-104603.

Fahrenthold, David A. 2014. "Senate Democrat's Reelection Pitch to Alaskans: I'm a Thorn in Obama's Side." *Washington Post*, July 13. Accessed March 15, 2015. http://www.washingtonpost.com/politics/senate-democrats-reelection-pitch-to-alaskans-im-a-thorn-in-obamas-side/2014/07/13/a6a7c60e-083a-11e4-aodd-f2b22a257353_story.html.

Faltin, Pamela. 2014. *Concord Monitor*, April 15, Opinion section.

Faucheux, Ronald. 2002. *Running for Office*. New York: M. Evans.

Fenno, Richard F. 1978. *Home Style*. Boston: Little Brown.

Ferraro, Thomas, and Rachelle Yonglai. 2013. "House Republicans Divided on Immigration Reform." *Reuters*, July 10. Accessed April 30, 2015. http://www.reuters.com/article/2013/07/11/us-usa-immigration-idUSBRE9690QD20130711.

Fine, Terri Susan, and Aubrey Jewett. 2008. "Promoting Civic Engagement and the College Student Poll Worker Study: Who Works the Polls on Election Day?" Paper presented at the American Political Science Association Teaching and Learning Conference, San Jose, CA, February 2008.

Fiorina, Morris P. 1978. "Economic Retrospective Voting in American National Elections: A Micro-Analysis." *American Journal of Political Science* 5 (1): 426–43.

———. 1981. *Retrospective Voting in American National Elections*. New Haven, CT: Yale University Press.

Fitzgerald, Jay. 2011. "Massachusetts vs. New Hampshire." *Boston Globe*, August 21.

Folke, Olle, and James M. Snyder. 2012. "Gubernatorial Midterm Slumps." *American Journal of Political Science* 56 (4): 931–48.

Fox, Lauren. 2014. "Why Florida's 13th District Special Election between David Jolly and Alex Sink Matters in March: The Special Election in Florida's 13th District Could Make or Break Obama Care Legacy in the Midterm." *U.S. News and World Report*, January 15. Accessed March 15, 2015. http://www.usnews.com /news/articles/2014/01/15/why-floridas-13th-district-special-election-between -david-jolly-and-alex-sink-matters-in-march.

Freelander, David. 2014. "New Hampshire Says 'No' to Interloper Scott Brown." *Daily Beast*, November 4. Accessed June 1, 2015. http://www.thedailybeast.com /articles/2014/11/04/new-hampshire-says-no-to-interloper-scott-brown.html.

Fuller, Jaime. 2014. "Obamacare Will Likely Help Republicans in 2014. But, 2016 Is a Different Deal." *Washington Post*, April 28. Accessed March 14, 2015. http:// www.washingtonpost.com/blogs/the-fix/wp/2014/04/28/do-republicans -benefit-from-obamacare-in-2014-maybe-but-it-isnt-likely-to-help-them-in -2016/.

Gallup. 2015. "State of the States, 2014." http://www.gallup.com/poll/125066/State -States.aspx.

Gamson, William and Kathryn Lasch. 1983. "The Political Culture of Social Welfare Policy." In *Evaluating the Welfare State: Social and Political Perspectives*, edited by S. Spiro and E. Yuchtman-Yarr. New York: Academic Press.

Gamson, William, and Andre Modigliani. 1989. "Media Discourse and Public Opinion on Nuclear Power: A Constructions Approach." *American Journal of Sociology* 95 (1): 1–37.

Gardner, Cory. 2014. "Next Generation Energy." Cory Gardner for Senate, September 1. Accessed April 18, 2015. https://www.youtube./com/watch?v= NPKzyophmNw.

Gelman, Andrew, and Jennifer Hill. 2007. *Data Analysis Using Regression and Multilevel/Hierarchical Models*. New York: Cambridge University Press.

Gerber, Alan S., Gregory A. Huber, Daniel R. Biggers, and David J. Hendry. 2014. "Ballot Secrecy Concerns and Voter Mobilization: New Experimental Evidence about Message Source, Context, and the Duration of Mobilization Effects." *American Politics Research* 42 (5): 896–923.

Gerber, Alan S., Gregory A. Huber, David Doherty, and Conor M. Dowling. 2013. "Is There a Secret Ballot?: Ballot Secrecy Perceptions and Their Implications for Voting Behaviour." *British Journal of Political Science* 43 (1): 77–102.

Gilbert, Katie. 2014. "Could a GOP Congress Back Renewable Energy?" *Institutional Investor*, December 24. http://www.institutionalinvestor.com/article /3413224/banking-and-capital-markets-corporations/could-a-gop-congress -back-renewable-energy.html#.VU4uxNVhHw.

Gimpel, James G., and Kimberly A. Karnes. 2005. "The Rural Side of the Urban-Rural Gap." *PS: Political Science & Politics* 39 (3): 467–72.

Gitlin, Todd. 1980. *The Whole World Is Watching*. Berkeley: University of California Press.

Glueck, Katie. 2014. "Tom Harkin: Joni Ernst as Pretty as Taylor Swift? So What?" *Politico*, November 2. Accessed March 14, 2015. http://www.politico.com/story /2014/11/2014-iowa-elections-tom-harkin-joni-ernst-taylor-swift-112433.html.

Godbout, Jean-François. 2013. "Turnout and Presidential Coattails in Congressional Elections." *Public Choice* 157 (1/2): 333–56.

Goidel, Kirby. 2014. "2014: Louisiana Survey." LSU Public Policy Research Lab.

Goldstein, Kenneth M., and Mathew J. Dallek. 2014. "Was It a Wave? What Does It Mean?" *Forum* 12 (4): 627–38.

GOP. 2013. "Bruce Braley's Convenient Conversion on ObamaCare." https://www .gop.com/bruce-braleys-convenient-conversion-on-obamacare/.

Green, Donald P., and Alan S. Gerber. 2004. *Get Out the Vote*. Washington, DC: Brookings Institution Press.

Gronke, Paul. 2014. "Voter Confidence as a Metric of Election Performance." In *The Measure of American Elections*, edited by Barry C. Burden and Charles Stewart III. New York: Cambridge University Press, 248–70.

Haddadin, Jim. 2013. "Scott Brown Says His Family Roots Go Back Nine Generations in New Hampshire." *PolitiFact New Hampshire*. December 20.

Hainmueller, Jens, and Daniel J. Hopkins. 2014. "Public Attitudes toward Immigration." *Annual Review of Political Science* 17: 225–49.

Hajnal, Zoltan L., and Taeku Lee. 2011. *Why Americans Don't Join the Party: Race, Immigration and the Failure (of Political Parties) to Engage the Electorate*. Princeton, NJ: Princeton University Press.

Hajnal, Zoltan L., and Michael U. Rivera. 2014. "Immigration, Latinos, and White Partisan Politics: The New Democratic Defection." *American Journal of Political Science* 58 (4): 773–89.

Help America Vote Act. 2002. Public Law 107–252. https://www.gpo.gov/fdsys/pkg /PLAW-107publ252/content-detail.html.

Herron, Michael C., and Daniel A. Smith. 2015. "Precinct Closing Times in Florida during the 2012 General Election." *Election Law Journal* 14 (3): 220–38.

———. 2016. "Precinct Resources and Voter Wait Times." *Electoral Studies* 42: 249–63.

Highton, Benjamin. 2006. "Long Lines, Voting Machine Availability, and Turnout: The Case of Franklin County, Ohio in the 2004 Presidential Election." *PS: Political Science & Politics* 39 (1): 65–68.

Hillygus, D. Sunshine, and Todd Shields. 2008. *The Persuadable Voter: Strategic Candidates and Wedge Issues in Political Campaigns*. Princeton, NJ: Princeton University Press.

Hinckley, Barbara. 1980. "House Reelections and Senate Defeats: The Role of the Challenger." *British Journal of Political Science* 10 (4): 441–60.

Holan, Angie Drobnic. 2013. "Lie of the Year: 'If You Like Your Health Care Plan, You Can Keep It.'" *Tampa Bay Times*, December 12. Accessed March 14, 2015. http://www.politifact.com/truth-o-meter/article/2013/dec/12/lie-year-if-you -like-your-health-care-plan-keep-it/.

Hopkins, Dan. 2014. "All Politics Is Presidential." *FiveThirtyEight*, March 17. Accessed June 1, 2014. https://fivethirtyeight.com/features/all-politics-is -presidential/.

Huey-Burns, Caitlin. 2014. "In Arkansas, It's Tom Cotton vs. Barack Obama." *Real Clear Politics*, September 29. Accessed September 30, 2014. http://www. realclearpolitics.com/articles/2014/09/29/in_arkansas_its_tom_cotton_vs _barack_obama_124115.html.

Huntington, Samuel P. 2004a. "The Hispanic Challenge." *Foreign Policy* (March/ April): 30–45.

———. 2004b. *Who Are We? The Challenges to America's National Identity*. New York: Simon and Schuster.

Hurley, Jeff. 2014. "Former State Legislators in Congress and White House." National Conference of State Legislatures, December 29. Accessed February 27, 2015. http://www.ncsl.org/ncsl-in-dc/publications-and-resources/former -state-legislators-in-congress.aspx.

Indiana Republican Party. 2014. "2014 Indiana Republican Party Platform." June 7. Accessed August 27, 2016. http://www.indgop.org/sites/default/files/2014 %20Platform-%20FINAL.pdf.

Institute for Energy Research. 2014. "U.S. Overtakes Saudi Arabia and Russia as Largest Oil Producer." July 10. Accessed May 2, 2015. http:// instituteforenergyresearch.org/analysis/u-s-overtakes-saudi-arabia-russia -worlds-biggest-oil-producer/.

Itkowitz, Colby. 2014. "Brown Campaign: Massachusetts Gaffe Was Not a Gaffe." *Washington Post*, July 16. Accessed March 17, 2015. https://www .washingtonpost.com/blogs/in-the-loop/wp/2014/07/16/brown-campaign -massachusetts-gaffe-was-not-a-gaffe/?.

Kamberis, Tom. 2014. "Desperate Republicans." *Concord Monitor*, April 14.

Kapur, Sahil. 2014. "Four Reasons the GOP Has a Huge Advantage in the 2014 Elections." *Talking Points Memo*, February 20. Accessed May 2, 2015. http:// talkingpointsmemo.com/dc/the-huge-republican-advantage-2014-midterm -elections.

Kim, Seung Min, and Burgess Everett. 2014. "Democrats Push for Immigration Delay." *Politico*, September 10. Accessed September 11, 2014. http://www .politico.com/story/2014/09/immigration-delay-democrats-110836.

Kinder, Donald R., and Wendy Kam. 2012. *Us Against Them: Ethnocentric Founda- tions of American Opinion*. Chicago: University of Chicago Press.

Kinder, Donald R., and Lynn Sanders. 1996. *Divided by Color: Racial Politics and Democratic Ideals*. Chicago: University of Chicago Press.

Koger, Gregory, and Matthew J. Lebo. 2012. "Strategic Party Government and the 2010 Elections." *American Politics Research* 40 (5): 927–45.

Krogstad, Jens Manuel, and Mark Hugo Lopez. 2014. "5 Takeaways About the 2014 Latino Vote." Pew Research Center. November 10. Accessed May 1, 2015. http:// www.pewresearch.org/fact-tank/2014/11/10/5-takeaways-about-the-2014 -latino-vote/.

Krueger, Curtis. 2014. "Alex Sink Won't Challenge David Jolly for District 13 Seat in November." *Tampa Bay Times*, April 15. Accessed March 15, 2015. http://www .tampabay.com/news/politics/national/sink-will-not-run-for-congress-against -jolly-in-fall/2175148.

Jackson, Robert A. 2000. "Differential Influences on Participation in Midterm versus Presidential Elections." *Social Science Journal* 37 (3): 385–402.

Jacobson, Gary C. 2009. *The Politics of Congressional Elections*. New York: Longman.

———. 2013. *The Politics of Congressional Campaigns*. 8th ed. New York: Pearson.

———. 2015. "Obama and Nationalized Electoral Politics in the 2014 Midterm." *Political Science Quarterly* 130 (1): 1–25.

Jacobson, Louis. 2014. "Kay Hagan Says GOP Rival Thom Tillis Called Obamacare 'A Great Idea.'" *PolitiFact*, April 22. Accessed March 14, 2015. http://www .politifact.com/truth-o-meter/statements/2014/apr/22/kay-hagan/kay-hagan -says-gop-rival-thom-tillis-called-obamac/.

———. 2016. "Yes, Donald Trump Did Call Climate Change a Chinese Hoax." *PolitiFact*, June 3. Accessed August 31, 2016. http://www.politifact.com/truth -o-meter/statements/2016/jun/03/hillary-clinton/yes-donald-trump-did-call -climate-change-chinese-h/.

Jaffe, Alexandra. 2013. "Landrieu Touts ObamaCare Fix in First Ad." *The Hill*, December 11.

Karpowitz, Christopher F., J. Quin Monson, Lindsay Nielson, Kelly D. Patterson, and Steven A. Snell. 2011. "Political Norms and the Private Act of Voting." *Public Opinion Quarterly* 75 (4): 659–85.

Khimm, Suzy. 2012. "Obama Is Deporting Immigrants Faster Than Bush: Republicans Don't Think That's Enough." *Washington Post*, August 27. Accessed June 3, 2013. http://www.washingtonpost.com/blogs/wonkblog/wp/2012/08/27/obama -is-deporting-more-immigrants-than-bush-republicans-dont-think-thats -enough/.

Kimball, David C. 2013. "Why Are Voting Lines Longer for Urban Voters?" http:// papers.ssrn.com/sol3/papers.cfm?abstract id=2255009.

Knoll, Benjamin R. 2012. "¿Compañero o Extranjero?: Anti-Immigrant Nativism among Latino-Americans." *Social Science Quarterly* 93 (4): 911–31.

Koch, Jeffrey W. 2000. "Do Citizens Apply Gender Stereotypes to Infer Candidates' Ideological Orientations?" *Journal of Politics* 62 (2): 414–29.

Kondik, Kyle. 2014. "Senate 2016: The Republican's 2012 Homework." Center for Politics, Sabato's Crystal Ball, December 1. Accessed May 7, 2015. http://www .centerforpolitics.org/crystalball/articles/senate-2016-the-republicans -2012-homework/.

Kramer, Gerald. 1970. "The Effects of Precinct-Level Canvassing on Voter Behavior." *Public Opinion Quarterly* 34 (4): 560–72.

Latino Decisions. 2012. "New Poll: Obama Leads Romney among Latinos in Key 2012 Battleground States." June 22. Accessed June 14, 2013. http://www .latinodecisions.com/blog/2012/06/22/new-poll-obama-leads-romney-among -latinos-in-key-2012-battleground-states/.

———. 2014. "Election Eve Poll—National Toplines." November. Accessed March 3, 2015. http://www.latinodecisions.com/2014-election-eve -poll/.

Lauck, Jon. 2014. Panel discussion, South Dakota Political Traditions Conference, Vermillion, SD, November 13.

League of United Latin American Citizens v. Perry 548 U.S. 399. 2006.

Leal, David L. 2014. "Immigration Policy Versus Immigration Politics: Latinos and the Reform Debate." In *Undecided Nation: Political Gridlock and the Immigration Crisis*, edited by Tony Payan and Erika de la Garza, 79–95. New York: Springer.

Leamon, Eileen J., and Jason Bucelato. 2015. Federal Elections 2014: Election Results for the U.S. Senate and the U.S. House of Representatives. Washington, DC: Federal Election Commission.

Leber, Rebecca. 2015. "It's Time to Remind Climate Change Deniers That Weather and Climate Are Different." *New Republic*, January 27. Accessed May 7, 2015. http://www.newrepublic.com/article/120860/conservatives-confuse-climate -weather.

Leiserowitz, A., E. Maibach, C. Roser-Renouf, G. Feinberg, and S. Rosenthal. 2016. *Politics and Global Warming, Spring 2016*. Yale University and George Mason University. New Haven, CT: Yale Program on Climate Change Communication. Accessed August 27, 2016. http://climatecommunication.yale.edu /publications/politics-global-warming-spring-2016/2/.

Levinson, Alexia, Abby Livingston, Emily Cahn, Kyle Trygstad, and Shira Center. 2014. "The Best Congressional Campaigns of 2014." *Roll Call*, last modified November 10, 2014. http://atr.rollcall.com/the-best-congressional-campaigns -of-2014/?dcz=.

Lopez, Mark Hugo, Ana Gonzalez-Barrera, and Jens Manuel Krogstad. 2014. "Chapter 4: Top Issues in This Year's Election for Hispanic Voters." Pew Research Center Hispanic Trends, October 29. Accessed April 17, 2015. http:// www.pewhispanic.org/2014/10/29/chapter-4-top-issues-in-this-years -election-for-hispanic-voters/.

Lopez, Mark Hugo, Jens Manuel Krogstad, Eileen Patten, and Ana Gonzalez-Barrera. 2014. "Latino Voters and the 2014 Midterm Elections." Pew Research Center Hispanic Trends, October 16. Accessed May 4, 2015. http://www .pewhispanic.org/2014/10/16/latino-voters-and-the-2014-midterm-elections/.

Maloy, Simon. 2014. "Another Obamacare Enemy Folds: Thom Tillis Says North Carolina Should Consider Expanding Medicaid." *Salon*, October 22. Accessed March 14, 2015. http://www.salon.com/2014/10/22/another_obamacare_enemy _folds_thom_tillis_says_north_carolina_should_consider_expanding _medicaid/.

Maskell, Jack. 2004. "Postponement and Rescheduling of Elections to Federal Office." CRS Report for Congress, October 4.

Masket, Seth. 2009. "Did Obama's Ground Game Matter?: The Influence of Local Field Offices during the 2008 Presidential Election." *Public Opinion Quarterly* 73 (5): 1023–39.

Matson, Marsha and Terri Susan Fine. 2006. "Gender, Ethnicity, and Ballot Information: Ballot Cue in Low-Information Elections." *State Politics & Policy Quarterly* 6 (1): 49–72

Mayhew, David. 1974. "Congressional Elections: The Case of the Vanishing Marginals." *Polity* 6 (3): 295–317.

Mayotte, Jim. 2014. "We Need Brown." *Concord Monitor*, June 1.

McBeath, Jerry, and Carl Shepro. 2015. "Alaska Senate Race (Mark Begich v. Dan Sullivan): Begich Swept Out with the Tide." In *The Roads to Congress 2014*, edited by Sean D. Foreman and Robert Dewhirst, chap 15. Lanham, MD: Lexington Books.

McCarter, Joan. 2014. "Scott Brown Locks Up Key Dead New Hampshire Republican Endorsement." *Daily Kos*, October 27.

McCarthy, Justin. 2014a. "As New Enrollment Period Starts, ACA Approval at 37 Percent." Gallup.com, November 17. Accessed March 14, 2015. http://www.gallup.com/poll/179426/new-enrollment-period-starts-aca-approval.aspx.

———. 2014b. "Obama's 'Strong Disapproval' Double His 'Strong Approval': Republicans Are More Likely to Strongly Disapprove Now Than in 2010." Gallup, August 28. Accessed February 28, 2015. http://www.gallup.com/poll/175529/obama-strong-disapproval-double-strong-approval.aspx?.

McDonald, Michael P. 2010. "Voter Turnout in the 2010 Midterm Election." *Forum* 8 (4): 1–8. Accessed May 1, 2015. doi: 10.2202/1540-8884.1406.

———. 2014. "National General Election VEP Turnout Rates, 1789–Present." United States Election Project, June 11. Accessed March 14, 2015. http://www.electproject.org/national-1789-present.

McDonnell, Tim. 2014. "Meet the Senate's New Climate Denial Caucus." *Mother Jones*, November 5. Accessed May 9, 2015. http://www.motherjones.com/blue-marble/2014/11/meet-new-climate-denier-caucus.

McKee, Seth C. 2010. *Republican Ascendancy in Southern U.S. House Elections.* Boulder, CO: Westview Press.

McKenna, Elizabeth, and Hahrie Han. 2014. *Groundbreakers: How Obama's 2.2 Million Volunteers Transformed Campaigning in America.* New York: Oxford University Press.

Meacham, Andrew. 2013. "U.S. Rep. C. W. Bill Young Dies at 82." *Tampa Bay Times*, October 18. http://www.tampabay.com/news/obituaries/congressional-legend-cw-bill-young-dies-at-82/2148018.

"Midterm Election Strategy: Republican Principles for American Renewal." 2014. *Fox News*, October 3. Accessed May 2, 2015. http://www.foxnews.com/opinion/2014/10/03/midterm-election-strategy-republican-principles-for-american-renewal/.

Miller, Gary, and Norman Schofield. 2008. "The Transformation of the Republican and Democratic Coalitions in the United States." *Perspectives on Politics* 6 (3): 433–50.

Minnesota Republican Party. 2014. "Republican Party of Minnesota—2014 Standing Platform." Accessed August 27, 2016. http://mngop.com/wp-content/uploads/2015/08/Platform.pdf.

Montanaro, Domenico. 2012. "Demographics show why I-4 Corridor is no Longer a Swing Area." *NBC News,* November 8.

Montgomery, David. 2014a. "(Almost) Blowing It in the Badlands." *Argus Leader* (Sioux Falls, SD), November 2. http://www.politico.com/magazine/story /2014/11/almost-blowing-it-in-the-badlands-112431_Page2.html# .VvQzlGcUVMs.

———. 2014b. "Will Rounds Start Using Negative Ads?" *Argus Leader* (Sioux Falls, SD), October 10. http://www.argusleader.com/story/davidmontgomery/2014 /10/09/will-rounds-go-negative/16984213/.

Mooney, Chris. 2015. "It's Official: 2014 Was the Hottest Year in Recorded History." *Washington Post,* January 16. Accessed May 7, 2015. http://www .washingtonpost.com/blogs/wonkblog/wp/2015/01/16/its-official-2014-was -the-hottest-year-in-recorded-history/.

Mukherjee, Elora. 2009. "Abolishing the Time Tax on Voting." *Notre Dame Law Review* 85 (1): 177–246.

Muro, Mark, Jonathan Rothwell, and Devashree Saha. 2011. "Sizing the Clean Economy: A National and Regional Green Jobs Assessment." Brookings Institution, July 13. Accessed May 11, 2015. http://www.brookings.edu/research /reports/2011/07/13-clean-economy.

National Council of State Legislatures. 2015. "Absentee and Early Voting," February 11. Accessed March 17, 2015. www.ncsl.org/research/elections-and-campaigns /absentee-and-early-voting.aspx.

National Exit Poll. 2014. *CNN Politics,* November 5. Accessed May 1, 2015. http:// www.cnn.com/election/2014/results/race/senate.

NBC News/Marist Poll. 2014. "Georgia." October 31. Accessed March 14, 2015. http://newscms.nbcnews.com/sites/newscms/files/georgia_october_31_2014 _annotated_questionnaire_nbc_news-marist_poll.pdf.

Neiman, Max, Martin Johnson, and Shaun Bowler. 2006. "Partisanship and Views about Immigration in Southern California: Just How Partisan Is the Issue of Immigration?" *International Migration* 44 (2): 35–56.

Nelson, Libby. 2014. "Republicans Now Have Historic Majorities in State Legislatures: That's a Really Big Deal." *Vox,* November 6. Accessed January 14, 2015. http://www.vox.com/2014/11/6/7164287/midterm-elections-2014-state -legislatures-governors-party-control.

Neuman, W. Russell, Marion R. Just, and Ann N. Crigler. 1992. *Common Knowledge: News and the Construction of Political Meaning.* Chicago: University of Chicago Press.

*New York Times.* 2013. "How Long It Took Different Groups to Vote," February 4. http://www.nytimes.com/interactive/2013/02/05/us/politics/how-long-it-took -groups-to-vote.html.

Noble, Jason. 2012. "Medicare Divides Candidates." *Des Moines Register,* September 23.

Obama, Barack. 2013. "Executive Order 13639: Establishment of the Presidential Commission of Election Administration." March 28.

———. 2013. "Remarks by the President in the State of the Union Address." February 12.

"Observations on Wait Times for Voters on Election Day 2012: Report to Congressional Requesters." 2014. *U.S. General Accounting Office*, Report #14-850, September 30.

O'Connor, Patrick. 2014. "Top 2014 Ad Themes: Obama, Local Issues, but No Shutdown." *Wall Street Journal*, September 24. Accessed February 28, 2014. http://blogs.wsj.com/washwire/2014/09/24/top-2014-ad-themes-obama-local -issues-but-no-shutdown/.

O'Donoghue, Julia. 2014. "Mary Landrieu, Bill Cassidy, Rob Maness Spar in First Louisiana Senate Debate." NOLA, October 14. Accessed May 9, 2015. http:// www.nola.com/politics/index.ssf/2014/10/cassidy_landrieu_shreveport_de .html.

O'Gorman, Mark. 2014. "Natural Uncertainty: Reconciling the Contrasting Environmental Goals of America's First Natural Security President—Barack Obama." In *The American Election 2012: Contexts and Consequences*, edited by Ward R. Holder and Peter B. Josephson, 171–86. New York: Palgrave.

Olabisi, Ugbedor and Nwonye Chukwunoso. 2012. "Modeling and Analysis of the Queue Dynamics in the Nigerian Voting System." *Operations Research Journal* 6: 9–22.

OnTheIssues.org. 2015. "Mark Pryor on Health Care." Accessed September 14, 2016. http://www.ontheissues.org/Social/Mary_Pryor_Health_Care.htm.

Ostermeier, Eric. 2014. "Which States Have the Longest and Shortest Election Day Voting Hours?" *Smart Politics*, Humphrey School of Public Affairs, University of Minnesota, July 10. Accessed June 6, 2017. http://editions.lib.umn.edu /smartpolitics/2014/07/10/which-states-have-the-longest/.

Panagopoulos, Costas. 2011. "Voter Turnout in the 2010 Congressional Midterm Elections" *PS: Political Science and Politics* 44 (2): 317–19.

Parenti, Michael. 1993. *Inventing Reality: The Politics of News Media*. 2nd ed. New York: St. Thomas Press.

Parker, Ashley, Nick Corasaniti, and Erica Berenstein. 2016. "Voices from Donald Trump's Rallies, Uncensored." *New York Times*, August 3. Accessed August 14, 2016. http://www.nytimes.com/2016/08/04/us/politics/donald_trump -supporters.html.

Peoples, Steve. 2014. "Brown Faces History, Residency Questions in NH Bid." *Huffington Post*, February 27. Accessed September 1, 2015. http://www .huffingtonpost.com/huff-wires/20140324/us-scott-brown/.

Persily, Nathaniel. 2014. *The American Voting Experience: Report and Recommendations of the Presidential Commission on Election Administration*. Accessed March 15, 2015. https://law.stanford.edu/index.php?webauth-document =publication/466754/doc/slspublic/Amer%20Voting%20Exper-final%20draft %2001-04-14-1.pdf.

Peters, Jeremy. 2013. "Waiting Times at Ballot Boxes Draw Scrutiny." *New York Times*, February 4, A1.

Pettigrew, Stephen. 2013. "Time Tax: Which Groups Wait in the Longest Lines on Election Day?" Accessed March 15, 2015. http://scholar.harvard.edu/files /pettigrew/files/waiting_times_to_vote_paper.pdf.

Pew Research Center. 2013a. "Public's Views on Human Evolution." December 30. Accessed May 10, 2015. http://www.pewforum.org/2013/12/30/publics-views -on-human-evolution/.

———. 2013b. "GOP Deeply Divided over Climate Change." November 1. Accessed May 10, 2015. http://www.people-press.org/2013/11/01/gop-deeply-divided -over-climate-change/.

———. 2014. "Compare Political Typology Groups: Obama Approval." June 26. Accessed May 4, 2015. http://www.people-press.org/2014/06/26/typology -comparison/obama-approval/.

———. 2015. "Congressional Favorability." March 29. Accessed May 4, 2015. http:// www.pewresearch.org/data-trend/political-attitudes/congressional -favorability/.

Plumer, Brad. 2012. "GOP Platform Highlights the Party's Abrupt Shift on Energy, Climate." *Washington Post*, August 30. Accessed May 6, 2015. http://www .washingtonpost.com/blogs/wonkblog/wp/2012/08/30/gop-platform -highlights-the-partys-drastic-shift-on-energy-climate-issues/.

Powers, Scott, and David Damron. 2013. "Analysis: 201,000 in Florida Didn't Vote because of Long Lines." *Orlando Sentinel*, January 29.

"President Obama's Acceptance Speech (Full Transcript)." 2012. *Washington Post*, November 7. Accessed March 15, 2015. https://www.washingtonpost.com /politics/decision2012/president-obamas-acceptance-speech-full -transcript/2012/11/07/ae133e44-28a5-11e2-96b6-8e6a7524553f_story.html.

Presidential Commission on Election Administration. 2014. The American Voting Experience: Report and Recommendations of the Presidential Commission on Election Administration. January.

Ragsdale, Lynn, and Jerrold G. Rusk. 2011. "Casting Votes: The National Campaign Context and State Turnout, 1920–2008." *Political Research Quarterly* 64 (December): 840–57.

Real Clear Politics. 2014. "Polls: Obama and Democrats' Health Care Plan." Accessed March 14, 2015. http://www.realclearpolitics.com/epolls/other /obama_and_democrats_health_care_plan-1130.html.

Richardson, Nathan, Madeline Gottlieb, Alan Krupnick, and Hannah Wiseman. 2013. Resources for the Future, *The State of State Shale Gas Regulation*. May 1. Accessed May 5, 2015. http://www.rff.org/rff/documents/RFF-Rpt -StateofStateRegs_Report.pdf.

Rodden, Jonathan. 2010. "The Geographic Distribution of Political Preferences." *Annual Review of Political Science* 13: 297–340.

Rogers, Alex. 2014. "Midterm Elections See a Surge in Ads About Energy and Environment." *Time*, September 23. Accessed February 28, 2014. http://time .com/3421833/2014-midterm-elections-energy-environment/.

Rouse, Stella M., Betina Cutaia Wilkinson, and James C. Garand. 2010. "Divided
      Loyalties?: Understanding Variation in Latinos' Attitudes toward Immigra-
      tion." *Social Science Quarterly* 91 (3): 856–82.
Rubin, Jennifer. 2014. "Obama's Immigration Train Wreck." *Washington Post*,
      September 7. Accessed May 1, 2015. http://www.washingtonpost.com/blogs
      /right-turn/wp/2014/09/07/obamas-immigration-train-wreck/.
Saenz, Arlette. 2014. "Americans for Prosperity Unleashes Another Attack on Mark
      Pryor." *ABC News*, April 1. Accessed March 14, 2015. http://abcnews.go.com
      /blogs/politics/2014/04/americans-for-prosperity-unleashes-another-attack
      -on-mark-pryor/.
Sauter, Michael B. 2013. "The 10 Most Oil-Rich States." *USA Today*, August 3.
      Accessed May 11, 2015. http://www.usatoday.com/story/money/business
      /2013/08/03/the-most-oil-rich-states/2613497/.
Schor, Elena. 2014. "KEYSTONE XL: Obama Admin Announces Further Delay for
      Pipeline Project." *EENews*, April 18. Accessed May 4, 2015. http://www.eenews
      .net/stories/1059998154.
Schudson, Michael. 2003. *The Sociology of News*. New York: W. W. Norton.
Shear, Michael D. 2014. "Obama Delays Immigration Action, Yielding to Demo-
      cratic Concerns." *New York Times*, September 6.
Shelby County v. Holder 570 U.S. _____ .2013.
Sides, John, and Lynn Vavreck. 2013. *The Gamble: Choice and Chance in the 2012
      Presidential Election*. Princeton, NJ: Princeton University Press, 2013.
Silber Mohamed, Heather. 2017. *The New Americans?: Immigration, Protest, and the
      Politics of Latino Identity*. Lawrence: University Press of Kansas.
Smith, Grant. 2014. "U.S. Seen as Biggest Oil Producer after Overtaking Saudi."
      *BloombergBusiness*, July 4. Accessed May 2, 2015. http://www.bloomberg.com
      /news/articles/2014-07-04/u-s-seen-as-biggest-oil-producer-after-overtaking
      -saudi.
Spencer, Douglas, and Zachary S. Markovits. 2010. "Long Lines at Polling Stations?:
      Observations from an Election Day Field Study." *Election Law Journal* 9 (1):
      3–17.
Spross, Jeff. 2014. "Iowa Senate Candidate Joni Ernst Joins the 'I Don't Know the
      Science' Chorus on Climate Change." *ThinkProgress*, September 29. Accessed
      May 10, 2015. http://thinkprogress.org/climate/2014/09/29/3573254/joni-ernst
      -science-climate.
"State of the Union 2013 Transcript." 2013. *Washington Post*, February 12. Accessed
      March 14, 2015. https://www.washingtonpost.com/politics/state-of-the-union
      -2013-president-obamas-address-to-congress-transcript/2013/02/12/d429b574
      -7574-11e2-95e4-6148e45d7adb_story.html.
Stein, Sam. 2014. "Some Clarity on What Mitch McConnell Wants for Kentucky's
      Obamacare Exchange." *Huffington Post*, October 27. Accessed March 14, 2015.
      http://www.huffingtonpost.com/2014/10/27/mitch-mcconnell-obamacare
      _n_6054850.html.

Stewart, Charles, III. 2013a. "2012 Survey of the Performance of American Elections." Accessed June 6, 2017. https://dataverse.harvard.edu/dataset.xhtml?persistentId=hdl:1902.1/21624.

———. 2013b. "Waiting to Vote in 2012." *Journal of Law and Politics* 28 (4): 439–63.

———. "2014 Survey of the Performance of American Elections, regular study." doi:10.7910/DVN/28979.

Stewart, Charles, III, and Stephen Ansolabehere. 2015. "Waiting to Vote." *Election Law Journal* 14 (1): 47–53.

Stirewalt, Chris. 2015. "GOP Gains Threaten Dems' National Power Source." *Fox News*, January 13. Accessed February 27, 2015. http://www.foxnews.com/politics/2015/01/13/gop-state-gains-threaten-dems-national-power-source/.

Stockley, Joshua. 2015. "Louisiana Senate Race (Bill Cassidy v. Mary Landrieu): Landrieu (D) v. Cassidy (R) and Maness (R) and Hollis (R) and Obama: The End of an Era in the Deep South." In *The Roads to Congress 2014*, edited by Sean D. Foreman and Robert Dewhirst, chap. 19. Lanham, MD: Lexington Books.

Sussman, Bob. 2014. "The US-China Climate Deal: Not a Free Ride for the Chinese." *Brookings Institution Blog*, November 25. Accessed May 9, 2015. http://www.brookings.edu/blogs/planetpolicy/posts/2014/11/25-us-china-climate-deal-sussman.

Taylor, Paul. 2012. "The Growing Electoral Clout of Blacks Is Driven by Turnout, Not Demographics." Pew Research Center: Social and Demographic Trends. December 26. Accessed May 1, 2015. http://www.pewsocialtrends.org/2012/12/26/the-growing-electoral-clout-of-blacks-is-driven-by-turnout-not-demographics/.

Tesler, Michael. 2016. "Trump Is the First Modern Republican to Win the Nomination Based on Racial Prejudice." *The Monkey Cage*, August 1. Accessed August 14, 2016. https://www.washingtonpost.com/news/monkey-cage/wp/2016/08/01/trump-is-the-first-republican-in-modern-times-to-win-the-partys-nomination-on-anti-minority-sentiments/.

Tesler, Michael, and David O. Sears. 2010. *Obama's Race: The 2008 Election and the Dream of a Post-Racial America*. Chicago: University of Chicago Press.

Texas Republican Party. 2014. "2014 Platform Final." Accessed August 27, 2016. https://www.texasgop.org/wp-content/uploads/2014/06/2014-Platform-Final.pdf.

Theiss-Smith, Elizabeth, and Richard Braunstein. 2005. "The Nationalization of Local Politics in South Dakota." In *Dancing without Partners: How Candidates, Parties, and Interest Group in the New Campaign Finance Environment*, ed. David B. Magleby, J. Quinn Monson, and Kelly Patterson. Provo, UT: Brigham Young University, Center for Elections and Democracy.

Thompson, Andrea. 2015. "Scorching July Is World's Hottest Month on Record." *Climate Central*, August 15. Accessed August 27, 2016. http://www.climatecentral.org/news/july-another-record-hot-month-20605.

Tichenor, Daniel. 2002. *Dividing Lines: The Politics of Immigration Control in America*. Princeton, NJ: Princeton University Press.

———. 2014. "The Congressional Dynamics of Immigration Reform." In *Undecided Nation: Political Gridlock and the Immigration Crisis*, edited by Tony Payan and Erika de la Garza, 23–48. New York: Springer.

Timm, Jane C. 2014. "GOP Senate Candidate Won't Answer on Climate Change." MSNBC, October 8. Accessed May 7, 2015. http://www.msnbc.com/gop-senate-candidate-wont-answer-climate-change.

Tom Cotton for Senate. 2014. "Cotton to Obama and Pryor: 'Time to Act on Keystone XL Pipeline,'" February 4. Accessed May 4, 2015. http://www.tomcotton.com/2014/02/ cotton-obama-pryor-time-act-keystone-xl-pipeline/.

Tuchman, Gaye. 1978. *Making News: A Study in the Construction of Reality*. New York: Free Press.

Tufte, Edward. 1975. "Determinants of the Outcomes of Midterm Congressional Elections." *American Political Science Review* 69 (3): 812–26.

Tunnell, Ted. 2006. "Creating 'the Propaganda of History': Southern Editors and the Origins of Carpetbagger and Scalawag." *Journal of Southern History* 72 (4): 789–822.

Tuohy, Dan. 2014. "GOP Hopes Dashed in Hard-Fought Race." *Union Leader* (Manchester, NH), November 5.

Turner, Jim. 2014. "Rick Scott: Ken Detzner Directed to Restore Voter 'Confidence.'" *Sunshine State News*, November 14. http://www.sunshinestatenews.com/story/rick-scott-ken-detzner-directed-restore-voter-%E2%80%98confidence%E2%80%99.

Tupper, Seth. 2014. "Poll: Rounds, Pressler Virtually Tied if Weiland Dropped Out." *Rapid City Journal*, October 6.

Univision. 2011. "Transcript of President Obama's Townhall." Univision.com, March 29. Accessed May 1, 2015. http://noticias.univision.com/article/351788/2011-03-29/educacion/noticias/transcript-of-president-obamas-townhall.

U.S. Bureau of Labor Statistics. 2014. "The Marcellus Shale Gas Boom in Pennsylvania: Employment and Wage Trends." February. Accessed March 14, 2015. http://www.bls.gov/opub/mlr/2014/article/the-marcellus-shale-gas-boom-in-pennsylvania.htm.

U.S. Commission on Civil Rights. 2001. "Voting Irregularities in Florida during the 2000 Presidential Election." June.

U.S. General Accounting Office Report. 2014. "Observations on Wait Times for Voters on Election Day 2012: Report to Congressional Requesters." Report #14-850. September 30.

U.S. Global Change Research Group. 2014. *Climate Change Impacts in the United States*. May. Accessed May 14, 2015. http://www.globalchange.gov/browse/reports.

Viser, Matt, and Andrea Estes. 2010. "Big Win for Brown: Republican Trounces Coakley for Senate, Imperils Obama Health Plan." *Boston Globe*, January 20. http://archive.boston.com/news/politics/2008/articles/2010/01/20/republican_trounces_coakley_for_senate_imperils_obama_health_plan/?page=2.

Wallace, Sophia J. 2012. "It's Complicated: Latinos, President Obama, and the 2012 Election." *Social Science Quarterly* 93 (5): 1360–83.

Wartman, Scott. 2014a. "McConnell: Don't Expect Much from Congress This Year." Cincinnati.com (*Cincinnati Inquirer*), March 7. Accessed May 9, 2015. http://www.cincinnati.com/story/news/politics/elections/2014/03/07/mcconnell-expect-much-congress-year/6170921/.

Wartman, Scott. 2014b. "McConnell Talks Brent Spence, Heroin, Ebola." Cincinnati.com (*Cincinnati Inquirer*), October 2. Accessed May 7, 2015. http://www.cincinnati.com/story/news/politics/2014/10/02/mcconnell-taking-ebola-threat-seriously/16586749/.

*Washington Post–ABC News.* 2014. "September 2014 Washington Post-ABC News Poll." September 9. https://www.washingtonpost.com/politics/polling/september-2014-washington-postabc-news-poll/2014/09/09/e09e1da2-37d5-11e4-a023-1d61f7f31a05_page.html.

Wasserman, David. 2013. "The GOP's Built-In Midterm Turnout Advantage." *Cook Political Report*, May 31. Accessed May 2, 2015. http://cookpolitical.com/story/5776.

"We Believe in America: Republican Platform." 2012. Republican National Convention 2012. Accessed August 27, 2016. https://prod-static-ngop-pbl.s3.amazonaws.com/docs/2012GOPPlatform.pdf.

The White House. 2012. "Remarks by the President at Univision Town Hall with Jorge Ramos and Maria Elena Salinas." Office of the Press Secretary, September 20. Accessed June 1, 2013. http://www.whitehouse.gov/the-press-office/2012/09/20/remarks-president-univision-townhall-jorge-ramos-and-maria-elena-salina.

Wolfinger, Raymond E., Steven J. Rosenstone, and Richard A. McIntosh. 1981. "Presidential and Congressional Voters Compared." *American Politics Quarterly* 9 (2): 245–56.

Wong, Cara, Jake Bowers, Tarah Williams, and Katherine Simmons. 2013. "Bringing the Person Back In: Boundaries, Perceptions, and the Measurement of Racial Context." *Journal of Politics* 68 (2): 386–96.

Wyatt, Kristen. 2014. "Senate Candidate Cory Gardner Touts a Failed Measure." *Denver Post*, September 4. Accessed April 19, 2015. http://www.denverpost.com/localpolitics/ci26468178/.

Yang, Muer, Michael Fry, David Kelton, and Ted Allen. 2014. "Improving Voting Systems through Service-operations Management," *Production and Operations Management* 23:1083–97.

Youngman, Sam. 2014. "McConnell's Latest Ad Targets Obama, Grimes on Coal." Kentucky.com (*Lexington Herald Leader*), July 18. Accessed May 5, 2015. http://www.kentucky.com/2014/07/18/3341840/mcconnells-latest-ad-targets-obama.html.

Yourish, Karen, Wilson Andrews, Larry Buchanan, and Alan McLean. 2013. "State Gun Laws Enacted in the Year Since Newtown." *New York Times*, December 10. Accessed February 27, 2015. http://www.nytimes.com/interactive/2013/12/10/us/state-gun-laws-enacted-in-the-year-since-newtown.html?.

YouTube. 2014a. "Brown, NH for Scott." Radio ad. Accessed June 1, 2015. https://www.youtube.com/watch?v=IS7RbSDKiK4.

———. 2014b. "Brown, Scott: A New Day," November 3. Accessed June 1, 2015. https://www.youtube.com/watch?v=Bj5NfUWUmbE.

———. 2014c. "Shaheen, NH First: Jeanne." Accessed June 1, 2015. https://www.youtube.com/watch?v=6Brc_9Y8aYQ.

———. 2014d. "Shaheen for Senate," June 24. Accessed June 1, 2015. https://www.youtube.com/watch?v=rRcwLSUjcTw.

Yulsman, Tom. 2016. "This Past July Was the Hottest of 1,639 Months on Record." *Discover Blog*, August 18. Accessed August 27. http://blogs.discovermagazine.com/imageo/2016/08/18/july-2016-hottest-such-month-on-record/.

Zipperer, Rachael. 2013. "What's in a Name?" *Georgia Political Review*, August 8. Accessed March 14, 2015. http://georgiapoliticalreview.com/whats-in-a-name-2/.

Zurcher, Anthony. 2014. "Obama Blasted for Immigration Delay." BBC, September 8. Accessed May 1, 2015. http://www.bbc.com/news/blogs-echochambers-29117066.